Reluctant Frontiersman

Photographic portrait of James Ross Larkin, taken about 1860.
This image was used on a carte-de-visite made at St. Louis.

Reluctant Frontiersman

*James Ross Larkin on the
Santa Fe Trail
1856–57*

Edited and Annotated by Barton H. Barbour

*Published in cooperation with
the Historical Society of New Mexico*

University of New Mexico Press

Albuquerque

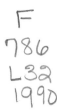

F
786
L32
1990

Library of Congress Cataloging-in-Publication Data

Larkin, James Ross, 1831–1875.
Reluctant frontiersman: James Ross Larkin on the Sante Fe Trail,
1856–57 / edited and annotated by Barton H. Barbour.—1st ed.
p. cm.
"Memorandum book of Jas. R. Larkin of St. Louis, Mo.": p.
"Published in cooperation with the Historical Society
of New Mexico."
Includes bibliographical references.
ISBN 0-8263-1183-0.—ISBN 0-8263-1208-X (pbk.)
1. Larkin, James Ross, 1831–1875—Diaries. 2. Pioneers—
Southwest, New—Diaries. 3. Sante Fe Trail. 4. Southwest, New—
Description and travel. 5. Frontier and pioneer life—Southwest,
New. I. Barbour, Barton H., 1951   . II. Larkin, James Ross, 1831–
1875. Memorandum book of Jas. R. Larkin of St. Louis, Mo. 1990.
III. Historical Society of New Mexico. IV. Title.
F786.L32   1990
979'.02'092—dc20
89-25073
CIP

To Vachel

Contents

Contents

Illustrations

Foreword

In May of 1987 President Ronald Reagan signed a congressional bill elevating the Santa Fe Trail to the status of a National Historic Trail, bringing it, for interpretive purposes, under the jurisdiction of the National Park Service. With the passage of that measure, the old pioneer route that had once linked the border state of Missouri with the frontier province of New Mexico gained some of the recognition and respect that is its just due.

In the annals of the American West, the story of the Santa Fe Trail forms a bold and dramatic chapter. The men and women who, for a variety of motives, braved the rigors of an overland journey to New Mexico were part of a floodtide of history that swept southwestward, becoming one arm of America's march toward the Pacific. Along this trail, travelers found profit, adventure, romance, and physical and spiritual renewal. But, at times, they also met with financial loss, unrelieved hardship, injury, and even death. To take the trail to Santa Fe, whether by ox train, muleback, or stagecoach, was always a calculated gamble, and that being the case inevitably there were winners and losers.

One of those who accepted the risks was James Ross Larkin, member of a prominent St. Louis family and an overlander categorized in his day as a health-seeker, that is, an individual seeking a cure in the salubrious West. In a small leather-bound book, he kept a diary of his experiences, and today his faithful recording furnishing us valuable insights into the history of the Santa Fe Trail during the middle 1850s.

On October 28, 1856, Larkin and his party passed the ruins of Bent's Old Fort, located on the north bank of the Arkansas River in southeastern Colorado. He could scarcely have imagined that the daily journal he was keeping would one day, in 1980, come back to this very place, donated by his great-grandson to the National Park Service, which restored the fort and now administers it as a National Historic Site. It was there, as he tells us in his Introduction, that Barton H. Barbour chanced upon the diary, recognized its merits as a historical document, and obtained permission from the Park Service to edit and publish it.

Although many health-seekers made the trip to New Mexico—Josiah Gregg being the best-known among them—few left accounts of their experiences and impressions. Larkin's jottings, therefore, assume added importance. In a series of carefully researched introductory chapters, Barbour places the diary in the context of the times, providing a summary of Larkin's background and his life after returning from Santa Fe and giving an analysis of his character and motives. This material adds significantly to an understanding of the diary.

In his descriptive bibliography, *Platte River Road Narratives* (1988), Merrill J. Mattes lists more than two thousand first-hand accounts, published and unpublished, by emigrants who traveled the central route to Oregon and California. The number of such narratives for the Santa Fe Trail is far smaller, and hence each one has proportionally larger value in expanding and refining our knowledge of this subject. So, we can be grateful that Mr. Barbour not only made his discovery of the Larkin diary, but that he devoted an immense amount of time to bringing it to light in the

Foreword

present form. The result is an admirable contribution to the literature of the Santa Fe Trail.

> Marc Simmons
> Past-President,
> Santa Fe Trail Association

The current officers and members of the Board of Directors of the Historical Society of New Mexico are: Spencer Wilson, president; Charles Bennett, first vice president; Austin Hoover, secretary; and M. M. Bloom, Jr., treasurer. The members of the Board are: John P. Conron, Thomas E. Chavez, Richard N. Ellis, John Grassham, John P. Wilson, Albert H. Schroeder, William J. Lock, Myra Ellen Jenkins, Susan Berry, Darlis Miller, Robert R. White, Robert J. Torres, Elvis E. Fleming, Mary Jane Garcia, and Andres Segura.

Acknowledgments

Historians almost invariably perform their research and writing alone, but no book appears that fails to reflect the talents and creative energies of many other people. During the course of this project, I was fortunate to have enjoyed the confidence and support of several individuals whose kind advice and assistance are here gratefully acknowledged. I also wish to thank those institutions whose contributions were crucial.

The National Park Service, especially Superintendent Jerry R. Phillips of Bent's Old Fort National Historic Site, graciously made available to me James Ross Larkin's manuscript diary and other materials for research and publication. The archival staff at the Jefferson Memorial, Missouri Historical Society, provided kind and cooperative assistance during the research phase of this undertaking and greatly expedited my work, while the State Historical Society of Missouri at Columbia provided several important Larkin letters from 1866. Research was partially funded by a grant from the Student Research Allocation Committee, University of New Mexico. Thanks also to the publications committee of the New Mexico Historical Society for helping to make this publication possible.

Acknowledgments

Special thanks are due to Richard W. Etulain for unstintingly giving me many hours of guidance from an already busy schedule during the preparation of this manuscript. Thanks also to professors Jane Slaughter and John L. Kessell for reading my manuscript and providing helpful comments. I would also like to thank David V. Holtby, of the University of New Mexico Press, whose patience and editorial advice are greatly appreciated. All errors of commission and omission remain, perforce, my own.

Barton H. Barbour
Albuquerque, N.M.
July 1989

Part One

James Ross Larkin and the Santa Fe Trail

I

Introduction

On the afternoon of September 25, 1856, twenty-five-year-old James Ross Larkin waited about three miles from the outskirts of bustling Westport, Missouri, the principal outfitting and debarkation point for travellers on the Santa Fe Trail. The small party included Larkin, his driver (a man identified only as "Hamilton"), and the far-famed but aging Indian trader and frontier entrepreneur William Bent, who had spent more than half of his forty-seven years on the plains. The men had made a final halt to await the impending delivery of two mules and a bushel of fresh apples, after which they would join the remainder of Bent's caravan, and take to the trail in earnest. While the three cooled their heels, Larkin's reflections must have included mingled excitement and anxiety as he eyed his new and costly "waggon" and harness, his saddle, and the heaps of assorted gear necessary to ensure a pleasant and comfortable prairie excursion.

Indeed, as his exhaustive inventory demonstrates, Larkin was most lavishly provisioned.[1] During the previous two

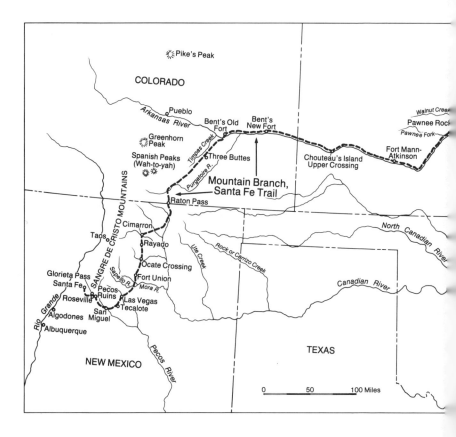

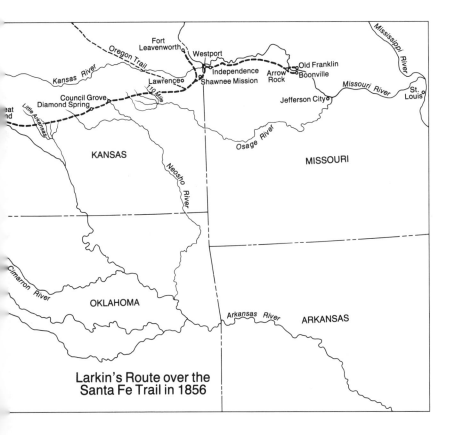

Larkin's Route over the
Santa Fe Trail in 1856

hectic days at Westport, he had purchased the bulk of his equipment, as well as a pair of mules and a horse, carefully recording in a small notebook each item with its value. Most of his trail gear, such as foodstuffs and cooking equipment, came from the establishment of J. & W. R. Bernard, prominent Westport outfitters. Larkin's fine "Finlay's ambulance" he had bought from Finlay & Doherty, carriage manufacturers located just a few doors from his home in St. Louis.[2] Because this was Larkin's first wilderness trail experience, he had undoubtedly required assistance in procuring the appropriate equipment and supplies. His cousins, Edward James and William Henry Glasgow (of the firm Glasgow & Brother), or his guide and patron, William Bent, each had more than sufficient experience with the Santa Fe Trail to have provided the requisite guidance for a "greenhorn" like Larkin.

He needed some good advice. Upon this prairie voyage might depend the quality of his health and the prospect of a longer life. Larkin's constitution was never altogether sound, and he was certainly a man who relished the comforts of hearth and home. Less than two weeks earlier, he had returned from an extended trip to the East intended to bolster his flagging health, but the sojourn failed to produce satisfactory results. Lodged in hotels and at the homes of family or friends, Larkin always travelled in comfort, if not in outright luxury. Certainly, he had never slept on the open prairie in the company of bullwhackers and Indian traders. But perhaps there was virtue in such an undertaking. He had heard about other young men in St. Louis for whom the "prairie cure" proved successful. Besides, his prosperous mercantile family was more than willing to subsidize the venture and would also provide him access to important men in New Mexico. After all, he counted among his

kinsmen some of the wealthiest and most politically important men in St. Louis. Although he felt uneasy about ven-
turing alone into the "wilderness," he mollified his fears
about the risks and discomfort inherent in prairie travel with
the hope for renewed health. In the end, Larkin's desire for
better health overshadowed his resistance, and compelled
him to inaugurate his health-seeking odyssey in 1856.

Whether Larkin nursed literary pretensions, or recognized
the historical significance of his journey, or simply followed a
fashion of the day common among literate western travellers, he kept a diary that covers at least a portion of his
travels and experiences. The small black leather-bound
notebook containing his daily entries serves as the principal
element of the present work.[3] Larkin's diary discloses much
more than a monotonous recapitulation of mileage and
weather, details that often comprise the chief characteristic
of the genre. A critical analysis of his diary's contents opens a
window, albeit with the shade partly drawn, on the "interior" James Ross Larkin that tells us something about the individual on the trail, and helps to illuminate the social, intellectual, and economic networks that bound mid-
nineteenth-century St. Louis to its distant dependency—
Santa Fe.

Like the carriage that safeguarded his material possessions
from damage during the plains journey, Larkin's diary provided security for his private thoughts and a sanctuary for his
cultural and intellectual baggage. Compensation and conso-
lation for the fact that he was far removed from his family
and friends, the diary may have served an important function as a source of self-definition for him. Through the
medium of his diary, he maintained a continuous link with
his past and built a bridge to his future.

Larkin was no pathfinder. Rather, he was a reluctant frontiersman who lacked the relentless drive so often associated with bold explorers. But there were to be thousands of men like him in the West, and only a few like Jedediah Smith or John Charles Frémont. The family wealth and connections with businessmen in New Mexico that distinguished Larkin from the average overland traveler provided him with the means and the opportunity to record a unique view of life on the trail and in Santa Fe. Essentially, James Ross Larkin's diary tells the story of an obscure young gentleman health-seeker on the Santa Fe Trail; but beyond this, I believe that several significant features of the diary may be noted. It is perhaps the most extensive account of a health-seeker on the trail, and it is an important addition to primary literature that bears upon the Santa Fe Trail and New Mexico in 1856–57. It is the story of one of the many anonymous men on the Santa Fe Trail who never attained high positions in government or commerce, but who still played an important role in the Americanization of the Southwest. Larkin's journal entries during the weeks of travel from Westport to Bent's Fort shed new light on William Bent's life during the twilight years of his career in the Indian trade at Bent's New Fort.[4] No other diarist known to me has left any account of life on the trail with William Bent. Larkin spent an entire month with Bent and his Cheyenne wife, Yellow Woman. Later, at Santa Fe, James quickly established himself among the leading American merchants and military men, and his diary describes many aspects of daily life at the territorial capital and its environs during 1856–57. Finally, James Ross Larkin's diary can be examined as a case study to weigh the validity of some of our notions about young men's Western experiences during the nineteenth century.

The Santa Fe Trail has attracted the attention of popular and scholarly writers for well over a century. Henry Inman's *The Old Santa Fe Trail* (1897), the first extensive postmortem account of the trail, established the standard for other dramatic and romanticized narrative histories. Roughly similar but updated treatments would appear for successive generations of readers.[5] Drawing from first-hand accounts by William Becknell, Thomas James, George C. Sibley, Josiah Gregg (himself the trail's first historian), James Josiah Webb, and others, historians customarily emphasized the early years of trail life and the trade with New Mexico, or the exciting confrontations with Indians along the route in the 1860s and later.[6] This predisposition to focus on the march of empire and Indian-white conflicts has contributed to historians' neglect of an important phase of the early territorial period: the decade of the 1850s.[7]

Information for the social history of the "inter-bellum" period is found chiefly among primary sources in archives, newspapers, and published contemporary diaries, memoirs, and books. Crucial to this study were additional Larkin diaries and correspondence that came to light in archival repositories. Research also revealed genealogical and other data on his family, and pertinent details concerning some of the persons and events that figure in his narrative. Contemporary newspapers from Santa Fe and St. Louis provided excellent raw materials from which to recreate the sociocultural milieu of James's life in St. Louis and subsequent activities in the Southwest. Considering how diligently historians have mined newspapers of the period, it is surprising that while Larkin's name was printed twice in the *Santa Fe Weekly Gazette* in connection with affairs on the trail, he has appeared in no published source on the Santa Fe Trail that I have examined.

Several important published works contain material useful in reconstructing Santa Fe Trail social history during the 1850s. Alexander Majors's narrative of the freighting industry during the years following the American acquisition of New Mexico yields much useful information, while memoirs by Marian Russell (and Susan Shelby Magoffin for the "year of decision," 1846) shed light on Anglo women's experiences on the trail to New Mexico. The best contemporary work on New Mexico during the fifties is W. W. H. Davis's *El Gringo: or, New Mexico and Her People* (1857). Davis was United States attorney for the territory (1853–57), and his book is a thorough, if biased, account.[8] Two additional books useful in recreating Larkin's Santa Fe are memoirs by territorial governor David Meriwether and trader Franz Huning.[9]

Larkin's journal chronicles one individual's perception of Western travel and must be distinguished from works by Gregg, Majors, and others who wrote for publication. Davis's *El Gringo*, for example, abounds with richly detailed passages about life in New Mexico, while Larkin's rather laconical diary registers his impressionistic responses to his first Western trek. Both works reflect an amalgam of popular notions and their writers' personalities, but Davis's editorializing was calculated to inform and influence a wide audience, and Larkin's diary written during spare moments on the trail and in Santa Fe was never edited or revised. Moreover, it was intended for no other purpose than his own edification, or perhaps that of his family and friends.

Genesis Of The Project

This project began to take shape in 1984, while I was employed as a museum technician at Bent's Old Fort National Historic Site. While cataloging a historical collection consisting mostly of objects on display at the reconstructed adobe trading post, I was delighted to discover that an original manuscript diary had somehow found its way into the collection. The leather-bound journal, measuring four inches by six inches, and about one-half inch in thickness, contained the diary of a heretofore unknown Santa Fe Trail traveler. Larkin's trail diary, along with a carte-de-visite and some minor additional materials, was initially loaned to the National Park Service in 1979 by his great-grandson, Phillip D. Beall, Jr., a retired lawyer then living at Pensacola, Florida. In 1980 the Larkin materials were donated to the Park Service. The small collection was forwarded to the Denver Regional Office and subsequently placed at Bent's Old Fort N.H.S., where it reposed in a safe for several years.

In 1984 the National Park Service kindly granted my request for permission to transcribe and edit the manuscript diary with the ultimate goal of making it available to a larger readership. The diary alone is of considerable significance to Santa Fe Trail studies, but additional biographical and other materials establishing its historical context will augment its utility for scholars. Research conducted intermittently over the next three years, chiefly at the Missouri Historical Society in St. Louis, resulted in the recovery of several other Larkin diaries, and important letters and business records, all of which have been integrated into the work presented here.

Editorial Note

I have transcribed James Ross Larkin's diary with a view to preserve all original spelling and punctuation and still provide a readable manuscript. Larkin's spelling is only slightly erratic, and should present no serious challenge to the reader. Words that Larkin wrote and then immediately crossed out are included in brackets, and later additions or modifications to entries are duly noted. Editorial intrusions have been kept to a minimum in order to present the reader with the diary as it was written. The original diary was not paginated but the transcription has been paginated to allow notes to be keyed to diary pages. Superscript numerals in the text indicate annotations to the diary, which appear as endnotes in a separate section.

Persons figuring prominently in the events noted in the diary are identified where possible, and additional appropriate background information is provided. Concerning military personnel that Larkin mentions, I have found two books edited by Robert W. Frazer to be especially useful: *New Mexico in 1850: A Military View* (Norman: University of Oklahoma Press, 1968), and *Mansfield on the Condition of the Western Forts* (Norman: University of Oklahoma Press, 1963). Rather than repeating data given by Frazer, I ask the reader to consult his books for information on officers mentioned only in passing by Larkin.

Larkin's detailed inventory and a list of men in the West to whom he carried letters of introduction will be found in an appendix, as will the Glasgow brothers' letter of introduction to Webb & Kingsbury, three newspaper articles extracted from the *Santa Fe Weekly Gazette* that mention Larkin or shed light on his activities at Bent's New Fort, and four letters written in 1866 in which Larkin discusses a possible trip to the plains.

Portrait of Mary Chambers Larkin, made about 1860.

St. Louis, *April 8th* 1857.

Mess Webb and Kingsbury Santa Fe

Bought of THOS. H. LARKIN & CO.,

WHOLESALE GROCERS AND COMMISSION MERCHANTS,

No. 30 LEVEE, Corner of Olive Street.

This is the only known surviving receipt of Thomas H. Larkin & Co., of St. Louis. Thomas was James' father, and this sale went to James Josiah Webb & John M. Kingsbury, business partners in Santa Fe from 1854–1861.

T R A N S A T L A N T I C   S K E T C H E S.

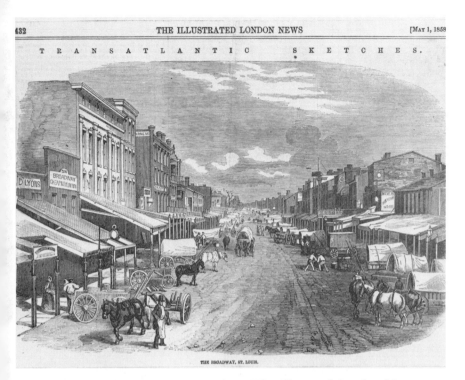

THE BROADWAY, ST. LOUIS.

"The Broadway, St. Louis," from *The Illustrated London News* (1858), shows the appearance of downtown St. Louis at the time James Ross Larkin went to New Mexico.

Memorandum Book
of
Jas R. Larkin
of St Louis Mo

Being on a trip from
St Louis to Bents Fort
& other points in the
west.

September
1856

Title page of James Ross Larkin's diary.

List of articles purchased
for the trip — & prices

1 Buffalo Robe	7	00
1 India Rubber cap	5	.
2 Pair Imp Blue Blankets	22	.
3 Pair W.S. Boots	17	50
1 " Shoes	3	50
2 " Shirts, 1 Pillow		
2 Pillow cases		
1 Military over coat	17	.
2 Pair Thick Pantaloons		
1 " Black do		
2 two Heavy coats		
4 Heavy Red flan Shirts		
3 Calico Shirts		
3 Hickory do		
4 Pair Red flan Drawers		
6 " Socks		
1 Saddle Blankets	1	50
1 Pistol Belt		
1 bar Black lead for camp		

1 Finlay Ambulance	202	00
1 Pair Hames & traces	25	00
2 Mules	325	00
1 Horse	100	00
1 Saddle	25	00
1 Bridle with 2 Bits	7	.
1 Pair Holsters	7	50
2 Long Straps 6 ft		75
1 Pair Spurs	1	50
2 Mow Bed cords		
1 Knife Scabbard		30
1 Gun Strap		
3 Picket Ropes 30 ft ea		
1 Pistol Colts Army Revolver	29	.
1 " Small Pocket	17	50
1 Hawkins Rifle	28	.
1 double Bbl Shot Gun		
1 Bullet Pouch	1	25
1 Shot do	2	25
1 Bullet Ladle		
3 " Moulds		
1 Jar caps & Straps		70

(*above*) Diary pages from October 12 and 13, 1856, when Larkin arrived at Bent's New Fort.

(*top right*) Page from the Webb & Kingsbury ledger book listing James Ross Larkin's purchases from the Santa Fe company during 1856–57.

(*bottom right*) John A. Scholten's photographic studio in St. Louis about 1870.

Dr. James R. Larkin Cr.

1856				1856				
Nov 22.	To Sales	440	3 00	Dec 10	By Cash	60	5 00	
" 27.	"	443	2 00	Feb 11 1857	" "	63	24 44	
Jan 22.	" "	467	20 31					
" 30. "	" "	471	4 13					
			29 44				29 44	
Feb 12	To Sales	476	3 25	Mar 5	By Cash	65	14 75	
" 19 "	" "	479	75					
" 24 "	" "	480	10 75					
			14 75				14 75	

Dr Judge K. Benedict Cr

1858				1859				
Dec 1	To Sales	740	8 00	Jany 1	By Cash	93	575 00	
" 3 "	"	741	2 25	" 24	" "	94	225 00	
" 11 "	"	742	12 25					
" 15 "	"	744	12 50					
" 20 "	"	746	6 00					
" 24 "	"	748	12 25					
1859 Feby 11 "	"	763	4 00					
" 22 "	Cash	94	50 00					

D.P.Rowland, Prest
Geo. H. Morgan, Sec.

Union Merchants Exchange

SECRETARY OFFICE

St Louis Jany 26 1875

Mrs James R. Larkin
                    Madame
                              The Merchants
members of this Exchange who had known
your late husband long and well, desiring to Express their sorrow at his loss
and the Esteem in which he was held
by them; to-day adopted resolutions, a
Copy of which I Enclose.
                              Be assured
Madame they Express the real sen-
timents of his fellow members, as
well as those of
                              Your obst Servt
                                        Geo H Morgan
                                              Secy

Letter of condolence from the Union Merchants Exchange, of
which Larkin was a member, to his widow following his death
on January 24, 1875.

2

"In Search of Better Health"

James Ross Larkin was born at Wilmington, Delaware, on July 23, 1831, into a family of sturdy Scots whose New World roots already reached back for more than a century. His mother, Susan Ross Glasgow (1811–1881), was also born in Delaware, probably at Christianna Bridge.[1] Susan's family lived briefly in Missouri, but upon her mother's death she returned to Wilmington where she received a Quaker education.[2] There she remained, and on April 20, 1830, was married to merchant Thomas Henry Larkin, the son of William Larkin, also of Wilmington.[3] In 1837, when the eldest son, James, was about six years old Thomas and Susan moved from Wilmington to St. Louis where they, and James, remained for the balance of their lives.

Saint Louis was a booming commercial center with a rapidly increasing population, and it already displayed in abundance emblems of contemporary municipal expansion. The city boasted a modest street railway, several theatres, the beginnings of a gas company, and a new German-language newspaper. William Carr Lane, who had been the first mayor of St. Louis (1823), was again in office in 1838. Related by marriage to the Larkins, he would one day be appointed the second governor of New Mexico Territory. Perhaps Larkin's knowledge of Lane's experiences in New Mexico during 1852–53 would influence his own decision to venture to Santa Fe in 1856. In any event, with a growing family to provide for, and probably aided to a degree by his wife's relatives, the Glasgow brothers, Thomas H. Larkin launched a business that eventually made him a very wealthy man.[4]

Thomas was an astute and enterprising merchant; by 1850 Thomas H. Larkin & Company had become one of the leading commission houses in St. Louis, with hemp raised locally for the New Orleans market as its mainstay in trade.[5] Ancillary interests of the concern included sales of goods destined for Santa Fe and for the fur trade of the upper Missouri country.[6] These sideline activities of Larkin & Co. would yield valuable contacts for James Larkin's future Santa Fe excursion. Especially important were James Josiah Webb and John Kingsbury, of the largest and best-known firm trading in Santa Fe. Thomas H. Larkin & Co. was located during 1854–55 at 53 North Front, which also served as the family residence. Until 1860, the Larkins lived in what was then, as now, the heart of downtown St. Louis. As a youngster Larkin would have been familiar with many of the store fronts in his neighborhood. Glasgow & Bro.'s wholesale operation was at 50 Levee, between Locust and Vine, while Finlay & Doherty's carriage factory, Laflin & Smith's gunpowder business, and Samuel Hawken's gunshop were each within a few blocks. Years later, when making preparations for his western trip, Larkin conducted business with merchants he probably had known for years, thanks to his father's business and residence location.

Thomas H. Larkin gained success rapidly after entering business at St. Louis, although he may previously have made a substantial amount of money in Delaware. In 1841 he bought what appears to have been the first of many city lots. These he would develop as income property, both residential and commercial.[7] By the time he died his real estate holdings included a large lot at Lucas (later, Locust) Place and 16th Street, an industrial lot at 518 North Main, and three cemetery plots in St. Louis, as well as two parcels of land in Brooklyn, New York.[8] A very capable and respected businessman, Thomas H. Larkin died on July 5, 1883, roughly two years after his wife, Susan. Both died at St. Louis and were buried at Bellefontaine Cemetery, the ultimate symbol of social standing in St. Louis.

Of the eight children born to Thomas and Susan, James Ross Larkin, named after his maternal grandparents, was the eldest. James remained relatively anonymous throughout his life, unlike his brothers Eli Hilles (1839–1920) and Thomas Henry (1848–1901) who would be remembered as leading businessmen of St. Louis.[9] James had four sisters: Anna, Margaret Lewis Foote, Mary Cuthbert, and Susan Glasgow. Anna, born in 1836, lived for only six years and died of scarlet fever in January [?] 1843, when James was eleven.[10] Margaret Lewis Foote was born in 1842 and died in 1863, just one month short of her twenty-first birthday.[11] James's youngest sister, Susan Glasgow, was just five when he went to New Mexico.[12]

Among James's sisters, only Mary Cuthbert (1844–1910) is directly related to the present work. Mary, despite protests from some members of her pro-southern family, married Dr.

David Lynn Magruder at St. Louis on October 15, 1862. Surgeon Magruder was a Union officer during the Civil War and probably made a lifelong career in the military, for he had attained the rank of general by the time of his death in 1910. Surprisingly, James Larkin had met and socialized with Magruder during his Santa Fe trip in 1856–57.[13] The record is not definitive on this point, but it seems that the friendship that developed between these two men may have led eventually to Dr. Magruder's introduction and subsequent marriage to Larkin's sister Mary.

Unlike brother Eli, James would never be eulogized for his philanthropy or brilliant business career. But each Larkin child received the benefit of a better than average education, probably at St. Louis, which had numerous nonsectarian and parochial academies, for girls as well as boys, and several colleges and universities. Larkin was literate and wrote in a reasonably clear and consistent hand. He seems also to have been conversant in French as well as his native English and had some understanding of German.

In the St. Louis City Directory for 1853, James's occupation is listed as "clerk," suggesting that he was not very deeply involved in the administration of his father's business. His fairly grave chronic ailments incapacitated him for the demands of a business career and relegated him to a quasi-dependent state for his entire life. When he departed for the West in 1856, James had already left the position of clerk and been promoted to a junior partnership in his father's business, as is indicated in his Santa Fe journal. On December 31, 1856, he writes, "This is the last day of my partnership in business with my father—the time (two years) [sic] having now expired."[14] It thus appears that the "partnership" with his father was in force as of January 1855. But Larkin's nagging health problems regularly imposed serious constraints on his activities, and the position was somewhat of a sinecure. A series of letters from Larkin to M. M. Broadwell of Kansas City, Missouri, during April and May 1866 indicates that Larkin was empowered to prosecute his father's business, but he may have routinely managed large cash transactions rather than brokering goods or overseeing large shipments.[15] Diary entries made later in his life, during 1869 and 1874, reveal that he seldom went to work in the city of St. Louis, though he maintained an office at his father's place of business. Instead, Larkin frequently remained at home while "Mr. L" (his father) took the train into the city to work. Then, too, from 1869 (perhaps earlier) to 1874, Larkin kept a notebook with city lot plats and accounts of rents received from numerous unrelated families in St. Louis, suggesting that he served an important function as the administrator of the family's extensive real estate holdings.[16]

Unfortunately, no details illuminating Larkin's childhood and youth are known. The earliest record I was able to examine is his Santa Fe Trail diary of 1856–57. A careful analysis of this document yields glimpses into his life before the trip to New Mexico. The style and tone of the diary, the subjects chosen, and relative attention allotted to each, are artifacts of Larkin's character and personality. At age twenty-five, for example, he was unmarried and still looked to his immediate family for security. He especially depended on his mother for guidance. She appears on the first page of the diary, "desiring" him to go out on the plains, and she assists in his preparations, making certain that he carries a Bible, along with some "excellent advice such as a mother can give." Larkin mentions his father and siblings less frequently, but clearly he misses his family, and is very pleased to receive letters from home. He also expresses sorrow over being unable to serve as "1st groomsman" at his cousin Edward James Glasgow's wedding, although one is not sure if it is the marriage or the "new suit" that James misses most.[17]

Understandably, James's poor health often occupies his attention. The trail diary includes references to self-administered medicine and notes on his condition, which often shifts dramatically from day to day. Indeed, in each of the three known diaries that Larkin kept, ill health—either his own or his family's—provides a dominant social theme. Some readers might be inclined to dismiss his daily concern, at times verging on obsessive, about his health as merely the carping of an effete hypochondriac dandy. Still, the variety of complaints to which he refers in the trail diary makes one wonder that he managed the trip at all. "Heroic" is too effusive a word to describe this sickly gentleman from St. Louis, but more than a mother's wish would be required to send most people into the wilderness. Perhaps a more realistic assessment of Larkin's character is that he would have, like Bartleby the Scrivner, "preferred not to" go into an unknown and alien environment, but was compelled to do so in an increasingly desperate struggle against disease. Here was a wealthy, city-bred young man suffering almost constant discomfort and pain, willing to risk the uncertainties of life on the plains and the danger of getting caught in an Indian war—all in the hope of restored health. Larkin's diary provides sufficient evidence of the symptoms besetting him to offer a tentative diagnosis of his ailments, and this matter is treated in a subsequent section (See Chapter 4).

Like his diary, the single extant photographic portrait of Larkin provides a sense of his character. The image is an albumin print carte-de-visite made around 1860 by John A. Scholten, who kept a studio at the corner of Fifth and Olive streets not far from where Larkin lived. The unretouched integrity inherent in the photographic image augments what can be gleaned of Larkin's personality from his diary. Taken a few years after he returned from New Mexico the portrait depicts a meticulously groomed and dapperly attired young man, bewhiskered according to the fashion of the times. Rather slightly built, his delicately featured handsome face is framed by dark hair and punctuated with watery light-colored eyes. James's portrait projects sensitivity, intelligence, and a measure of resolution. These characteristics comport with the personality that emerges from his diaries.[18]

About one year after Larkin's return from his Western journey, the Larkins celebrated an event that would shape his remaining years. On October 18, 1859, he wed an attractive young woman, Mary Chambers, of the important Chambers-Mullanphy family, longtime residents of St. Louis city and county.[19] When she was seventeen, Mary had been wed to a Dr. Robert Walters, of nearby St. Geneviève, Missouri. Tragically, only one month after her wedding, the doctor expired suddenly at the home of his parents. Seven years later, she married Larkin. Circumstances of their courtship are not known, but the wedding ceremony took place at the downtown home of her parents, on Broadway, near the gleaming, domed city courthouse. The Larkins left immediately for a honeymoon tour of Europe.

Following their return from the European holiday in 1860, James and Mary took up residence at the "southwest corner of 16th and Lucas Place," the location of a recently completed spacious and beautiful dwelling built for Thomas H. Larkin. Eventually, fashionable families left the downtown area "for the new suburbia west of Grand Avenue," and the mansion was purchased in 1886 (four years after Thomas H. Larkin died) by the Missouri Historical Society for $15,000.00. It became the first official home of that organization, which occupied it between 1887 and 1913.[20]

During his years with Mary, James gradually became a regular churchgoer. Though James was already a nominal Catholic, he seems not to have been particularly devout until after his marriage. At any rate, at least one newspaperman applauded Mary's mending of her husband's spiritual being, for he "was brought into the [Catholic] Church . . . due to the piety and good example of his wife." Nonetheless, James is known to have attended Mass while in Santa Fe.[21] He frequently attended church with his children, and on January 3, 1875, his daughter Magaret accompanied him to a High Mass for the last time in his life.[22]

The Larkin family provided sufficient wealth and income to guarantee a comfortable and secure existence, and Larkin's wife also brought substantial assets to the family's coffers. During 1869, Mary's mother gave each of her nine children parcels of city and country lots; Mary's portion was valued at over $100,000. Larkin wrote in his diary that Mary's mother, "Mrs. Jane Chambers [,] desiring to divide a portion of her property among her nine children, had it divided into nine parts, & today the drawing took place. . . . I drew share 'G,' being 20 [pieces] in town and 5 in country, valued at $110,000—an overvaluation." Not only did Larkin manage his wife's inherited real estate, but he also collected rents on properties that his father owned. For his services Larkin retained 25 percent of the gross receipts, while his father received the balance.[23]

The joys and sorrows of married life and rearing a family occupied Larkin for the fifteen years remaining in his life. Throughout those years he continued to suffer from chronic neuralgia and the discomforts of poor digestion. His 1869 and 1874 diaries reveal that these serious health problems did not prevent his taking great interest in his family as their lives progressed. The memory of his 1856 plains trip, however, or the influence of the western health legend lingered in Larkin's memory. Letters written in 1866 indicate that he contemplated another health-seeking trip to the plains, but if he made the journey, no record of it has survived.[24]

Larkin died following a bout with pneumonia on January 24, 1875, at the age of forty-three years and six months. Still a relatively young man, his weak health had finally played out; no longer would he enjoy the pleasures of time spent with his beloved family that formed the principal activity in his life. Inexplicably, during his last two weeks alive, and immediately preceding the fatal onset of pneumonia, James had occasion to refer to his Santa Fe Trail diary of nearly twenty years earlier. In some unused pages at the end of the trail journal he made a few final brief notations. Entries made for the first week of January 1875, like so many of his jottings, mostly concern the weather, and routine family matters. Possibly, as he wrote, he relived in his imagination that long ago journey one more time. Likewise, he must have reviewed his hopes and fears, his exhilaration and anxiety during the eventful prairie trip with William Bent and all the experiences that matured him as he broadened his acquaintance with the world around him.[25] Recollections of the fracas at Bent's Fort must surely have visited his consciousness as he once again committed his thoughts to the tattered day book that had chronicled his life's greatest adventure.

James Ross Larkin's funeral took place at St. John's Catholic church, on the corner of Sixth and Chesnut, squarely in the neighborhood in which he was nurtured, grew to maturity, and spent the bulk of his adult life. A St. Louisan from beginning to end, Larkin was laid to rest in beautiful

Bellefontaine Cemetery. Sadly, there at the graveside were his parents and his progeny, come to bid their last farewell to the most unlikely candidate among them to have ventured along the Santa Fe Trail to the Far West during the years when New Mexico, a mystery-shrouded colonial outpost of Missouri, was just beginning its lengthy territorial apprenticeship.

A more comprehensive biography of James Ross Larkin might have been possible but for fate's untimely intervention. Mary survived her husband by more than forty years and died in St. Louis on August 7, 1918, "at her country home, The Oaks, on the Chambers Road." Two decades later this beautiful house and its historic contents ("valuable oil paintings, antique furniture, china and other heirlooms") was completely gutted by fire. The conflagration of 1937 was doubly tragic, for not only was the irreplaceable mansion forfeited, but so too were papers and numerous family belongings that might have shed welcome additional light on Larkin's life.[26]

Of the eight children born to the Larkins during their years of marriage, six grew to maturity. The youngest son, James Ross, died at the age of ten years, and a daughter, Susan Ross, died in infancy. Thomas H. Larkin, Jr., named for James's father, ultimately moved to California, while Annie (born about 1866) married Wilbur Noell Beall—and subsequently, Charles W. Oliver—and lived in Pensacola, Florida. Margaret married John Rutherford Cooke, and Elizabeth married Benjamin Lewis. Two children seemingly remained unmarried: Jane Chambers Larkin, and Bartholomew Maziere Chambers Larkin. With the exceptions of Thomas and Annie, all of James and Mary Larkin's children lived at or near St. Louis. However, it is Annie's first marriage that bears upon the present work. A son born to Annie and Wilbur N. Beall, Phillip D. Beall, would in turn have a son named Phillip D. Beall, Jr., born about 1920. In 1934, while still a youth, he was the recipient of the eighty-year-old diary kept on the Santa Fe Trail by his great-grandfather, James Ross Larkin.[27] Nearly fifty years later, in recognition of the significance of the diary, Phillip D. Beall, Jr., donated it to the National Park Service.

3

St. Louis and Santa Fe: A Comparison in 1856

The St. Louis in which James Ross Larkin reached his majority would have been practically unrecognizable to St. Louisans of the previous generation. The brawling frontier town of six thousand in 1830 had matured; by 1856 more than 120,000 residents inhabited the limestone bluffs above the Mississippi. The demographic composition of the city, especially in its social and cultural dimensions, had been transformed during Larkin's first two decades of residence. St. Louis was now the most important Western commercial nexus, with a rapidly expanding urban population that dwarfed the earlier conglomeration of frontiersmen, soldiers, Indians, tradesmen, and a few wealthy merchants.

Many of the leading families were Creole descendents of the original inhabitants who continued to speak the French of their forbears and also preserved some of their traditions, as we shall see. But by 1830 a wave of European immigrants (chiefly German and Irish) as well as many new arrivals from the northern states were flooding into St. Louis, thereby

creating a chronic housing shortage and introducing substantial cultural modifications. In the years after 1830, the
German language would augment English, French, and
Spanish in the din heard down on the teeming levee. The
Larkin family came to St. Louis among the waves of new-
comers eager to take advantage of the greatly expanded
commercial opportunities that characterized the 1830s. By
1850 fully one-third of the city residents were German-
born. Indeed, so many residents spoke German that in September 1856 the Board of Public Schools considered introducing its study in the public school curriculum.[1] Higher
education also experienced robust growth during this period: Washington University came into being in 1857, and
Webster College entered into its fourth year of operation.[2]

While the cultural and demographic profiles of St. Louis
underwent dramatic alterations, so too did the city's economic structure. The two mainstays of early St. Louis business, furs and lead, no longer dominated as they had before
1830, though both still contributed significantly to the local
economy. Several major factors that militated for the diver-
sification of St. Louis commerce are worthy of mention. The
postwar crash of 1819, attending the War of 1812, led to a
realignment of economic priorities and brought an end to an
irresponsible "wildcat" era of town development. The 1822
Congressional dismantling of the United States Factory system, which held a monopoly on the Indian trade for more
than two decades, threw open a vast new field of endeavor to
St. Louis entrepreneurs. Also, as the Santa Fe trade bur-
geoned after 1821, St. Louis merchants made annual trips to
New York, Philadelphia, Baltimore, and elsewhere to purchase goods for the trade, and at the same time they solid-
ified commercial links with the east. Finally, St. Louis had
reaped, since 1826, the benefits of a considerable trade with

the army at Jefferson Barracks, which became the largest post in the nation during the 1840s. Trade with the troops and the government played an important role in boosting the local economy.

By 1850, more than any other city, St. Louis had become the "distributing center for Eastern goods on the Mississippi frontier and the dispatching point for Western produce to the outside world."³ Thomas H. Larkin was just one of many new commission merchants investing in St. Louis who moved immense harvests of corn, hemp, wheat, tobacco, and other commodities down to New Orleans or to eastern markets. The natural advantage of location made St. Louis ideally situated to emerge as a center of regional commerce, and steam power provided the decisive key to the transportation network. River transport made the city paramount among western cities by the mid-1830s, a primacy tellingly confirmed by the growing number of steamboats that docked at St. Louis each year. As a result, the levee fronting the river became the locus of frantic daily activity, with steamboats unloading and taking on cargoes amidst a babble of languages. The waterfront district was also the site of dozens of bordellos and dramshops that catered to the lawless and rowdy elements in St. Louis.

As the city of St. Louis modernized and urbanized, its rough backwoods appearance (excluding a scattering of palatial Creole mansions) gradually yielded to a more polished, uniformly cosmopolitan environment resembling other major American cities. Increased crime, housing shortages, political violence, ethnically based riots, and calamities such as epidemic cholera or fires plagued the urbanization of St. Louis, but other less traumatic displays of municipal evolution at least partially mitigated these aggravations. For example, the St. Louis Agricultural and Mechanical Association sponsored its first "Great Fair" in October 1856 to advertise the latest in tools, machines, and agricultural practices. Larkin found news of the event intriguing, but because he was in New Mexico at the time, could not attend. The agricultural fair became a regular feature of life in the city. By 1857 the city hall had been fitted with gas light, while several museums advertised a variety of exhibits of natural and man-made wonders, inevitably including a dinosaur skeleton and Egyptian mummies.[4] In addition, the Mercantile Library Association, established in 1845 to serve the intellectual community, exhibited in 1857 several "pieces of sculptured marble . . . exhumed from the ruins of Ancient Ninevah."[5]

Like other educated, cultured, and prosperous citizens, Larkin probably attended the Peoples' Theater or the St. Louis Theater, host to such luminaries as Sigismond Thalberg, an Austrian touted by some as the "greatest virtuoso pianist of the mid-19th century."[6] In March 1857 Larkin would miss an opportunity to see the celebrated exotic lecturer-adventuress, Lola Montez, who appeared at the St. Louis Theater. Meanwhile, the St. Louis Lyceum sponsored educational lectures and travelogues by visitors such as Bayard Taylor, one of the most widely read and popular American journalists of his day. Clearly, St. Louis enthusiastically displayed all the hallmarks of a nineteenth-century metropolis and its citizens took great civic pride in the rapid advances being made.

But still in evidence was a lively strain of the original French *mode de vivre* that provided an underpinning for an emergent character unique to St. Louis. The French heritage was amply reflected in the cadence of life, in domestic and civic architecture, in the continual round of socializing, and, certainly, in the local dialect. Naturally, the Gallic tradition was lodged most firmly in the Creole families of old St. Louis, who had established a cultural context for the city generally and a social context for the elite and aspiring that remained in force during the 1850s.[7]

Although obviously a wealthy and successful family, the Larkins probably would have been reckoned among the second or third rank of St. Louis families, the first rank being filled with worthies like the Saugrains, Soulards, Chouteaus, Lucases, Kennerlys, Bentons, and Clarks. The Glasgow family, however, related to Larkin through his maternal lineage, was not without influence and would certainly have acquainted the Larkins with some of the "best" families. After James's marriage to Mary Chambers, the Mullanphys and the Chamberses, also leading families, would in turn become part of the Larkin kinship network. As a result, the Larkins would have been welcome guests at some of the soirées and other goings-on that characterized elite life in St. Louis. William Clark Kennerly left a reminiscence of life in mid-century St. Louis that underscores the interconnectedness of social, political, and commercial ties among distinguished families. Indeed, during the 1860s the Larkins attended social gatherings at the home of Jefferson Kearny Clark, son of the famous explorer, William Clark. This was a compelling symbol of acceptance into the highest level of St. Louis society.[8]

Despite the convivial social atmosphere surrounding James in 1856, ominous clouds gathered on the horizon signifying frictions in American society that would burst into civil war just four years hence. During the summer of 1856 the movement to abolish slavery languished in most states, but in the Kansas Territory the issue took the center stage and raised a fury of contention that threatened to blaze into a bloody war. The Missouri press continually ran reports and editorials about the grave crisis threatening to engulf the Union. Larkin's diary entries for the first few days of his trip reflect his view of the growing unrest in Kansas.

Although Missouri was a slave state, the balance of pro- and anti-slave factions was about to tip in favor of the so-called Black Republicans, thanks partly to the new Irish and German populations. According to a city census of 1856, less than six thousand black men and women lived in the city and county of St. Louis. About 1200 were slaves and the remainder were free blacks. The Larkin family is believed to have owned two house slaves and was generally sympathetic to the South. They doubtless followed with keen interest the debate over slavery. Factionalism in Kansas Territory and the volatile slavery issue were inextricably entwined, and the furor spread to Missouri.

During September 1856 the steamer *Morning Star* (which boat, a week later, Larkin boarded for Kansas) arrived at St. Louis with the distressing news that Kansas was "in a state of insurrection."[9] Just a few days afterward, the editors of the *St. Louis Daily Missouri Democrat* wrote an essay to promote the "Great Fair" scheduled for October that inadvertently expressed what must have been a widely held, if naive, wish concerning the larger issue of black slavery: "After the distractions and gloomy forebodings and sectional exasperations which have grown out of a border war, *now we trust concluded* [original italics] . . . it is particularly pleasant to advert, by way of contrast, to the advances of science and the arts of life."[10] Meanwhile, B. M. Lynch advertised in both principal dailies for the purchase and sale of "Negroes on commission."[11]

Indeed, the famed Dred Scott himself lived in St. Louis intermittently, and few residents would have failed to observe with either alarm or hope the proceedings in the Scott case. On March 13, 1857, the *St. Louis Daily Missouri Democrat* carried its first notices on Justice Roger Brooke Taney's decision regarding Scott.[12] The daily press had for some time featured reports dealing with the difficulties in Bleeding Kansas, some tinged with near-hysteria, while Missourians in support of both sides crossed the border of Kansas to vote or fight.

Despite abolitionist rumblings and no shortage of matters of local concern in 1856, the citizenry of bustling St. Louis maintained very considerable ties with the West, and many of the city's businessmen were especially eager observers of western events. The daily newspapers of 1856–57 frequently carried reports on affairs in Kansas, California, Utah, New Mexico, and Mexico, often digested from other papers such as the *Santa Fe Weekly Gazette* or the *Kansas Enterprise*. The monthly Santa Fe-Independence mail service brought western tabloids to St. Louis which, in combination with the western freighting industry, provided a generally steady and reliable communication with Santa Fe. The golden age of western freighting, lasting roughly from about 1850 to 1875, was in full swing by 1856, when Larkin decided to take the trail to Santa Fe. In addition to the sprawling caravans of outfits such as Majors and Russell, many smaller trains were constantly in motion along the trail, a few of which Larkin encountered during his travels.

The Santa Fe Trail in 1856 was a busy thoroughfare, and even with the constant threat of Indian depredations, Mexicans, New Mexicans, and Americans alike found livelihoods on the trail either as employees or patrons of the trade. Some were second-generation traders, and many had made numerous crossings of the plains. The trade with Santa Fe had long been of special interest to St. Louisans, and the reverse was equally true. In 1793 Pedro Vial, a

Frenchman employed by Spain, had traversed the prairies separating the two towns. Efforts to establish a permanent connection antedated Vial's accomplishment by over half a century, as evidenced by the 1739 trade venture of the Mallet brothers. Although it was primarily a businessman's route, a number of tourists and health-seekers also went down the Santa Fe Trail. Commerce with Mexico and New Mexico was the chief objective for trail-minded men, but the enduring allure of the desert Southwest, and its climate, played an important secondary role. [13]

Unlike boom-town St. Louis, Santa Fe in 1856 appeared much as it had two hundred years earlier. At mid-century all of New Mexico slumbered, and another quarter-century would pass before the territory entered a rapid growth period. With a population of nearly five thousand Hispanos and a few hundred Anglo-Americans, mostly soldiers and traders, the town still retained the atmosphere of a foreign port at the terminus of a sea of grass. Although the initially tenuous American occupation of 1846 had been consolidated during the ensuing decade the town was, in the minds of most American commentators, rough, crude, dangerous, and decidedly alien in character and appearance. Even the army found conditions at Santa Fe too licentious for the maintenance of good order and in 1851 transferred headquarters of the Ninth Military Department to the more austere Fort Union, near Las Vegas. [14] In 1856–57 nearly two thousand soldiers served in New Mexico's Ninth Military Department, principally to overawe Indians and protect or escort freight caravans. Meanwhile, Fort Marcy, built during the Mexican War in 1846, had been abandoned and its ruins frowned above the city of Santa Fe. Santa Feans Frank Green and Thomas Bowler had purchased the old Fonda, and these two aggressive American entrepreneurs invited the "better class" of Americans (and presumably, New Mexicans) to patronize the hotel, which of course Larkin did. Other "American" lodgings were available, but the Fonda reigned as the preeminent gathering place for traders, soldiers, and tourists in Santa Fe.

The only recognizable examples of "American" architecture in town were the state house (today it is the Federal Court Building at Santa Fe) and the penitentiary, both then under construction, and neither to be finished for many years. These two pork barrels would produce years of easy profits for their promoters, "engineer" Joab Houghton and trader-turned-contractor Ceran St. Vrain.[15] The remainder of the "Villa Real de Santa Fé de San Francisco" consisted of single-story adobe houses, stores, and a few churches, clustered around the old plaza. The plaza itself was ringed with retail stores, mostly owned by Anglo-Americans, and the trade that continued every day—including Sundays—was the town's most characteristic activity. The ancient and decrepit Palace of the Governors dominating the north side of the plaza housed its most recent incumbent, Territorial Governor David Meriwether.

Apart from the governor and his retinue, and the traders and military men, a few other Anglo-American residents were engaged as lawyers, doctors, or newspaper men. There were the usual ne'er-do-wells, such as the Hispanic and Anglo-American gamblers plying their trade at the Fonda, augmented by a boisterous floating population of bullwhackers, clerks, and stage-line hands who continually thronged the monte tables found nearly everywhere in Santa Fe. Recently, however, the Placer Mining Company had imported quartz-crushing apparatus for use at the gold diggings south of Santa Fe, arguably the first tangible application of the Industrial Revolution to New Mexico. The company also brought a few men to work as operators and engineers at the mines.[16]

Scarcely any Anglo-American women found themselves in New Mexico. Those that did were military wives or daughters, along with a few traders' wives. Marian Russell, who later married a soldier, first entered New Mexico in 1852 and lived there intermittently during the next several years, leaving what has become, along with the diary of Susan Shelby Magoffin, one of the best accounts by a woman on the trail or in early territorial New Mexico.[17] James Ross Larkin's diary demonstrates that he enjoyed the familiar comforts of frequent socializing with the "American" ladies in town, but he also mingled with native New Mexican men and women, as did the officers and traders with whom he associated.

The majority of the approximately five thousand "Mexicans" of Santa Fe pursued farming or sheep ranching as they had for the past two centuries, while the remainder made their living as traders, artisans, prostitutes, or in the service trades. Wearing country-made clothing, and an occasional vividly colored Rio Grande or Saltillo serape, the average native male inhabitants elicited less commentary from Anglo visitors than did their feminine counterparts. The women's attire was judged, by conservative and prejudiced Missouri standards, both titillating and degenerate. Less ethnocentric than many of his countrymen, Larkin nevertheless found some of the customs of New Mexicans incomprehensible. And like many Anglo-American observers, he evinced a conviction of cultural superiority that occasionally surfaces in his diary.

Today we recognize that ethnic biases and presumptive cultural superiority informed, or warped, Anglo-American attitudes toward New Mexicans. Larkin's diary, and others, amply prove the case. However, just as Larkin and other "Gringos" in New Mexico perceived the native Hispanic and Indian cultures to be clearly different from their own, they were likewise misunderstood by New Mexicans. Observation of cultural differences was often registered in the form of derogatory superciliousness, common to Anglos and Hispanos alike.

By 1856 most of the New Mexican *ricos* displayed signs of acculturation to the Anglo model, for both men and women might be seen wearing the latest fashions from Baltimore or Philadelphia, via St. Louis of course. Indeed, beginning in about 1835 a few far-sighted wealthy New Mexicans had sent their male children to be educated at St. Louis so they might learn the ways of the "Gringos." But despite a huge demographic majority, unchallenged control of local politics, and significant activity in the Santa Fe and Mexican trades, New Mexicans did not often figure prominently in the principal contemporary chronicle of cultural and social matters in Santa Fe, the newspaper. Moreover, almost no mid-nineteenth-century New Mexicans kept diaries or journals like Larkin's (or few have appeared), leaving a large blank in the historical record and many unanswered questions.

Larkin's diary leaves the reader with an impression that the Anglo-American traders and officers existed in a self-contained world, largely separate from the native population, except for a few wealthy New Mexicans sympathetic to the "Americans." Similarly, Howard R. Lamar points out that the territorial government provided a republican veneer beneath which *patrones* were left free to dictate to their *peones* in the time-honored fashion of village administration. While the native population was thus occupied, Anglo-American merchants and lawyers assiduously bought

up land titles or sought profits stemming from federal lar-
gesse.[18] It seems that two distinct societies warily coexisted
for the first few years of the territorial era in New Mexico,
each ignoring the other as much as possible while seeking
opportunities in the new power structure. The conquerors
had won the province and no longer stood in fear of another
revolt, but the shift in sovereignty was more readily accom-
plished than the transformation of "Mexicans" into "Americans."

Anglo-Americans were zealously committed to the notion of progress, and they would have observed few encour-
aging signs of modernization in Santa Fe. No public schools
received funding in the Territory of New Mexico, nor were
there any city utilities, macadamized streets, or hospitals,
except one that the army operated. Native folk had long
since accommodated themselves to the lack of amenities,
although during the years before the American takeover
New Mexicans had repeatedly petitioned the Mexican government to ameliorate various problems. The early territorial period saw little change, in part because the Anglo-
Americans failed to construct a coherent administrative
structure to coordinate civilian, military, and Indian affairs.
Political infighting and confusion contributed to the per-
petuation of frontier conditions in New Mexico, the most
corrosive of which was the problem of continual Indian raids
throughout the territory.[19] Still, if the territorial capitol was
relatively unsophisticated and provincial, its native inhabitants could take pride in better than two centuries of history
and tradition that bequeathed to them a sense of "place"
denied most Anglo-Americans. But Larkin would have
been far more likely to be struck by the stark contrast
between Santa Fe and St. Louis, in appearance as well as in
culture.

Larkin arrived at Santa Fe from Bent's Fort on November 15, 1856, and stayed for about three months. After his disconcerting experiences with the Kiowas on the Arkansas, he was in the best possible frame of mind to appreciate conditions in the capitol. He refrained from denigrating the appearance of the town and was quite positively impressed with "the Fonda," which may be a reflection of his relief at having managed to escape the dangers of the wilderness and to gain the comparative security and safety of "civilization" in Santa Fe.

4

The Health Frontier
on the Santa Fe Trail

In his Santa Fe Trail journal Larkin frequently commented on his health disorders, and associated physical sufferings. The diary includes brief descriptions of his symptoms and measures taken to alleviate discomfort. Occasional appraisals of the relative virtues of Virginia or New Mexico climate suggest that he often reflected on the state of his health, or how best to improve it. At times his preoccupation with health was so dominant that he failed through neglect, or disability, to record much of what he observed. However, one needs to keep in mind an obvious but crucial point: a diary provides a secure environment in which its writer may air matters of personal concern that might not otherwise be discussed or recorded. The diary, therefore, provides the researcher an opportunity to probe the inner world of Larkin, though Larkin's particular interests and choices, as well as the nature of diary keeping itself, determine the amount and type of information conveyed. A brief summary of the western health frontier as Larkin knew it, and the role St. Louis played in the advance of that frontier, will help establish an appropriate context within which to discuss Larkin's maladies.

Larkin was by no means the first to risk his life for the possible benefits of a trip to the vaunted salubrious air of the Far West, but he did travel during the years when health-seekers on the overland trails were still relatively few. By 1856 a few doctors, travellers, and health-seekers had published books and articles heartily endorsing a Western excursion to produce relief or total recovery from even the most deadly afflictions, such as tuberculosis.[1]

At the time Larkin travelled to New Mexico, the health frontier of the Southwest was still in its infancy, and he took a place in the vanguard of the "gentlemen health seekers" who would ultimately throng such health resorts as Manitou or Colorado Springs by the 1880s. The Civil War imposed a temporary moratorium on all western development, but within the following decade dozens of published testimonials and propaganda pieces made possible the huge success of health resorts and hot springs in the mountain West.[2]

Poor health was endemic in the greater Mississippi valley during the early and middle nineteenth century, and the medical arts were wholly inadequate to meet the challenge. Ague (malaria), bilious fevers (dysenteries), consumption (tuberculosis), yellow fever, diphtheria, cholera, and smallpox were among the many torments that sent Missourians to early graves. So widespread was ill health in Missouri that a derogatory contemporary moniker, "Pukes," came to be applied to her residents. Cold, damp weather and poor housing made pneumonia and rheumatism distressingly familiar in St. Louis, where mortality rates from disease were unusually high. And wealth alone was insufficient to stave off the harvest of death, as the Larkin family knew. Physicians often could do little more than shrug their shoulders in resignation. For many conditions, a combination of pain killer and specifics (i.e., specific remedies) was administered for symptomatic relief until the patient either expired or improved. Wholesale unhealthfulness generated bountiful profits for homeopaths, allopaths, eclectics, and unscrupulous quacks at a time when medical licensing was practically nonexistent.

When all else failed, St. Louis doctors might acknowledge the limits of their skills by recommending a pilgrimage to the rejuvenative atmosphere of the Far West, especially to the Southern Plains, where disease and fevers were almost unknown, at least among whites.[3] St. Louisans deemed the plains climate eminently healthful, and many of them had fled to the Kansas prairies in 1849 to escape an outbreak of deadly cholera. Indeed, it is said that the original French settlers of Missouri would send their invalids either to the plains or the Rocky Mountains in search of a cure.[4]

Missourians were convinced that a trip to the plains, whether for prevention or cure, was likely to produce the desired affect. Several noted fur traders who lived in St. Louis had gone to the Rocky Mountains as "lantern-jawed shakers"—the bulk were tuberculars—and returned in robust health. Their accounts of miraculously restored health resulting from prairie travel circulated in the city and prompted other men with no interest in the fur trade to test the curative theory.[5] Health-seekers also joined the ranks of traders on the Santa Fe Trail shortly after the opening of the trade in 1821, and the route was conveniently located to tempt infirm St. Louisans. Moreover, when Josiah Gregg's *Commerce of the Prairies* appeared in 1844 it heralded the advent of overt health boosterism on the trail. A dozen years earlier, Gregg's own desperate gamble on the restorative qualities of prairie travel had paid off handsomely. He not only speedily recovered his health, but also discovered a new vocation as a Santa Fe trader.

Anyone reading Gregg's book would have been acquainted with his glowing account of the advantages of trail life.[6] *Commerce of the Prairies* enjoyed considerable popularity, and it is possible that Larkin read the book. In that event he would undoubtedly have been impressed by the author's enthusiasm for western travel, as well as by the notion that his own poor health might be improved if he followed Gregg's example. Imagine for a moment Larkin's reaction upon reading Gregg's effusive description of the "prairie cure":

Among the concourse of travellers at this "starting point," besides traders and tourists, a number of pale-faced individuals are generally to be met with. The Prairies have, in fact, become very celebrated for their sanative effects—more justly so, no doubt, than the most fashionable watering places of the North. Most chronic diseases, particularly liver complaints, dyspepsias, and similar affections, are often radically cured; owing, no doubt, to the peculiarities of diet, and the regular exercise incident to prairie life, as well as to the purity of atmosphere of those elevated, unembarrassed regions.[7]

Indeed, Larkin had already taken at least one trip in 1856 to "fashionable watering places," both in the North and in the South. His cousins, the Glasgows, may have owned a house at Cape May, New Jersey, but in any event, they frequented the same resort area through which Larkin travelled during his health-seeking trip to the east. He may also have visited other Glasgow family members who lived in Arkansas, near the most famous contemporary health-resort and hot springs.[8] However, neither the mountainous region of western Virginia, nor the seacoasts of New Jersey and Massachusetts effected a noticeable improvement in young Larkin's condition. Because renewed health had eluded his grasp Larkin, no doubt with his mother's encouragement, determined that he should make a trip to the plains, precisely as Gregg recommended. Even if Larkin did not read Gregg, or one of the few extant alternate sources, he greatly profited from his acquaintance with men who would have echoed Gregg's enthusiasm. It would be difficult to overstress the importance of Larkin's kinship ties with social and economic allies in the Glasgow family that facilitated preparations for his quest for health.

His cousins, Edward and William Glasgow, operated a commission house with substantial interests in the Santa Fe trade. Well known to James Josiah Webb and John M. Kingsbury, Dr. Henry Connelly, and other Santa Fe merchants, the Glasgows occasionally provided health-seekers "of abundant means" en route to New Mexico with letters of introduction to important Santa Feans.[9] The Glasgows probably wrote all of Larkin's letters of introduction to movers and shakers in the Territory of New Mexico, but only one, to Webb & Kingsbury, survives. At any rate, Larkin's perennially poor health was the prime determinant for his trip to New Mexico, and we turn now to a tentative diagnosis of his condition.

Like Josiah Gregg, James suffered from what was called "chronic dyspepsia," a common enough ailment, but difficult to define with precision. This indisposition may be analogous to gastroenteritis, or gastritis, both of which result from inflammation of the stomach or intestines. In addition, Larkin endured frequent bouts of neuralgia, another ill-defined malady that served as a nineteenth-century catch-all for problems related to the aftereffects of malaria, sustained exposure to cold or dampness, poor diet, and anxiety. Larkin's neuralgia was generally confined to his right leg, a condition referred to as sciatica, affecting the sciatic nerve, which runs from the hip to the foot. A nearly contemporary source indicates that "attacks of neuralgia are liable to recur, particularly when the general health is low, and some persons unhappily continue to suffer from occasional attacks during the greater part of their lifetime. . . . any source of pressure on the [sciatic] nerve within the pelvis, such as may be produced by a tumour, or even by constipation of the bowels, may excite an attack."[10]

The standard prescription for an attack of neuralgia or sciatica called for the ingestion of narcotics or alkaloids, principally opium, morphine, belladonna, or henbane. Larkin's inventory of trail equipage specifies one bottle of "pain killer," which a later diary entry identifies as paregoric, a camphorated tincture of opium, used to relieve diarrhea. Many preparations were widely employed, often in combination, in attempts to fight disease, giving rise to the term "puke and purge" cures. The concatenation of approved curatives must sometimes have wreaked appalling results in the patient's digestive system. Emetics caused vomiting, purgatives produced evacuation of the bowels, and opiates predisposed the user to constipation. Obviously, long-term ingestion of opiates would have opened the door to addiction, and Larkin, who resorted to such medications for two decades, may have developed at least a marginal dependence on paregoric or laudanum.[11] In his day, of course, opiate derivatives were considered standard—if not safe— remedies, and people of all ages and classes routinely ingested addictive pain killers. Even during the closing year of his life, Larkin's diary contains references to having taken "pills" or "oil" to relieve painful symptoms that continued to plague him.

In the course of his travels on the plains, Larkin's diary notes the incidence of neuralgia, constipation, and diarrhea, all more or less constant afflictions. While he may have experienced some temporary gains in his health as a result of the trip, in the end his condition probably was not greatly altered. Perhaps the dry air and high altitude of the southern plains proved more beneficial to sufferers of pulmonary disease than to invalids like Larkin. His optimism notwithstanding, Larkin suffered in Santa Fe just as he had at St. Louis, with no change in his condition apparent from his diary entries. Unfortunately, Larkin's Santa Fe diary abruptly ends before he returned in March 1857 to St. Louis, an ellipsis that will leave the matter, to a degree, forever unsettled. Evidence strongly suggests, however, that between March and July of 1857 Larkin made yet another round trip from Santa Fe to St. Louis.[12] In that case, one must conclude that even if prairie travel failed to work a permanent improvement in his health, at least he must have became inured to the rigors—or enamored of the rewards—of life on the plains, and decided to prolong his wanderings in spite of his condition.

5

The Trail to Santa Fe

The Santa Fe Trail as a Rite of Passage

The reasons one might embark on prairie travel varied according to the vocations and circumstances of those who undertook the venture. Profits attracted the merchant, and duty compelled the soldier, but what siren lured other travellers who eagerly volunteered and even paid for the opportunity to go out to the plains? For some, like Frederick Wislizenus—trail companions dubbed him "Whistling Jesus"—it was the quest for botanical and geological knowledge; for the infirm, such as Josiah Gregg, the high and dry Southwest seemed to offer strength and vigor; while for other wayfarers the quest for adventure or artistic inspiration was sufficient cause. "Gone to see the Elephant" was a phrase commonly used to describe the motivation of tourists whose object was simply to encounter exotic terrain and people in the West and survive to tell the tale back home among friends and family.[1]

In addition to these rationales for western travel Howard R. Lamar suggests in a provocative essay that for many young males the overland journey functioned as a rite of passage from adolescence to manhood.[2] But Lamar's study concerns young men associated with families on the Oregon-California trails whose experiences were fundamentally different from that of Larkin on his Santa Fe Trail journey. In Lamar's essay, the "passage" takes place within a mobile population whose members have made a deliberate effort to conserve social, legal, and behavioral conventions from the Eastern community, and to transport them intact through the wilderness to a new community in the West. Lamar finds that overlanders' caravans usually travelled under a covenant or code of regulations designed to "surround themselves with what was familiar and comforting," that the trains were not "outside the bounds of society," and that the "social contract" was not abrogated during the westward trek.[3] Such arrangements prevailed among the westering masses on the California-Oregon trails, but when specialized organization of Santa Fe caravans existed at all, it more often bore a military complexion meant to safeguard traders' goods, not social institutions.[4] Despite some substantial variations, however, either trail experience might have been important to a young man's maturation process.

Only one freighting outfit made a concerted effort to preserve proper Victorian institutions on the road to New Mexico while most traders, it seems, found a cultural crusade to be inexpedient or unwarranted. Alexander Majors and William Russell operated the largest freighting company on the Santa Fe Trail and the only outfit known to this writer to have drawn up rules of conduct. Majors, a puritanical zealot "opposed to all kinds of profanity," authored their famous "iron-clad" regulations.[5] In contrast,

Larkin's diary indicates that he travelled under no such strictures. His patron, William Bent, was a man who did not practice sabbatarianism, the proscription of travel on the Sabbath. Indeed, far from being a man of Christian forbearance and restraint, Bent was only too willing to resort to violence when he deemed it necessary, as Larkin's diary makes plain.[6] In addition, Larkin would have observed that William Bent and other cultural expatriots in the Southwest lived quite comfortably in two, even three, "worlds": those of the Anglo-American, the New Mexican Hispano, or the Indian. Larkin, himself a most proper gentleman, never commits to his diary a disparaging word about Bent or his Indian wife, suggesting that he found no impropriety in Bent's affinity with the aboriginal people and culture of the southern plains. Larkin could not entirely free himself from ethnic bias, but certainly he was less shrilly bigoted than many Missourians, and overlanders generally, who would more likely have dismissed Bent and his ilk as miscegenist "squaw men."

In another section of the essay, Lamar points out that overlanders generally considered Missourians to be "ignorant, brawling frontiersmen," "like hogs personified."[7] Quite unlike the mythic Missourian "ring-tailed roarers" on the California Trail, Larkin was upper-class, well-educated, single, and the product of an urban rather than agrarian upbringing. Lamar's profile of young men on the overland trail accommodates Larkin only at its most salient point: the trail experience was analogous to a rite of passage into manhood.

Larkin was patently a health-seeker, but his prairie travels may also be interpreted as a period of metamorphosis from youth to maturity. The sickly young urbanite could scarcely have based his decision to go to the plains on hard pragmatism alone. He could more easily have chosen to return to eastern health resorts, but he selected instead the trail to Santa Fe. Perhaps a spirit of adventure helped to shape his decision to travel with Bent's train, rather than take the faster and much less expensive monthly stage from Independence to Santa Fe. Although he occasionally groused about the danger and inconvenience of his trip, James accepted the challenge, and his action may well have become a catalyst that precipitated important self-discoveries, as we shall see.

Lamar likewise posits that young men between the ages of twenty-two and twenty-eight on the overland trail frequently developed close relationships with adult males other than their fathers and that such bonds facilitated the young men's adjustment to the world around them.[8] While a specific transformation is difficult to identify in Larkin's diary, his age and his relationship with William Bent would suggest that in these respects he conforms to Lamar's model. Manifest in the diary is that Bent was at least his protector, if not a mentor, until the time Larkin left Bent's New Fort en route to Santa Fe.

In spite of the reassuring presence of William Bent, Larkin may have sensed that the trail from St. Louis to Santa Fe led him also from childhood to adulthood. If he did experience a moment of stark self-realization, it could have occurred during the suspenseful night of October 14, 1856, as he lay awake in the heavily armed fort listening to the beating of Kiowa war drums outside the walls. That Larkin sought such a revelation is suggested in his diary entry for New Year's Eve 1856, when he writes: "Here I am away out in the wilderness, away from so many of the comforts &c. of city life at the close of this eventful year. How things change!"[9] At any rate, less than two years after his return to

St. Louis, Larkin had completed his passage to the "adult" phase of his life, symbolized by marriage and fatherhood.

The vacant expanse of prairie provided an ideal setting for Larkin's maturation. Removed as he was from his family circle, unencumbered by workaday cares, and deposited in an unfamiliar environment, Larkin perhaps sensed a new immediacy in each trail experience. When he departed aptly named Westport, Larkin left the familiar behind him and entered an exotic region whose physical and cultural landscape bears little resemblance today to what it was in 1856. The West remained for the majority of Americans a land conceived more in imagination than in experience and the characteristic imagery applied to the American West was as unsettled as the land itself.

As the American foothold in the southwestern territory became more firmly established, a handful of the first Anglo-Americans to have migrated to the southern plains and the former provinces of Mexico still clung to the vanishing lifestyle of the frontier trader. Kit Carson, Lucien B. Maxwell, and William Bent are typical of the men caught up in a transitional period that saw New Mexico transformed from an international frontier to an "American" settlement, from "unknown" to "known." Larkin's brief visit to New Mexico occurred at a time that heralded dramatic shifts in social and economic organization, and his diary reflects a blending of the familiar and the exotic that characterized Santa Fe in 1856–57, and continues to inform the region today.

Itinerary Of Larkin's Trail Experiences

St. Louis To Bent's New Fort James Ross Larkin left St. Louis on September 19, 1856, having made hasty preparations for his departure from Westport with a caravan belonging to

William Bent. He rolled out of St. Louis on the Pacific Railroad to Jefferson City, where he was to board the steamer *Morning Star,* known in the trade as "Tom Brierly's floating palace." Three days and several groundings later the *Morning Star* landed at Westport, or "Kansas." There, on September 25, Larkin joined Bent's caravan consisting of about sixteen men, along with Bent's Cheyenne wife, Yellow Woman, and a Pawnee youth under her care.

Shortly after the three wagons left Westport the men observed signs of the continuing border conflicts in Bleeding Kansas that presaged the coming Civil War. On September 27, Larkin passed through Lawrence, the Kansas headquarters of the quasimilitary Emmigrant Aid Company, whose operations consisted of bringing abolitionists, arms, and supplies into the territory. He noted houses burning "on account of the Kansas difficulties" and expressed fears for the safety of the party and its livestock. [10] But Bent's caravan was not molested and they moved westward, resting at most of the standard campsites on the trail.

On October 3 the party met two other gentlemen health-seekers en route to St. Louis who brought ill tidings of events at Bent's New Fort. Upon receipt of the news Larkin and Bent departed immediately for the fort to settle the difficulty. Larkin was present at the fort when word came of some troubles with the Cheyennes that would precipitate a punitive campaign in 1857 under the leadership of Colonel E. V. Sumner. Larkin noted on October 5: "Mr. B. informed [the Cheyennes] of the report that reached Sts. [states] before we started, that a number of their tribe had been killed & taken prisoner at or near Fort Laramie by the U.S. Troops, but they had not or pretended not to have heard of it, & looked quite serious on learning it."[11] From October 13 to 27 Larkin was quartered at Bent's New Fort, near present Lamar, Colorado, some thirty-five miles from the more famous Bent's Old Fort. During his sojourn at the fort Larkin witnessed a serious altercation between William Bent and one of his employees who had been giving whiskey to some Kiowas in violation of the law.[12] The argument might have ended in bloodshed but for the intervention of the Cheyennes, who prevented Bent from shooting the offender. Events at the fort reached a climax on October 14 when the Kiowas threatened to attack the fort, but a battle was avoided, and Larkin concluded to go on to Santa Fe as soon as was practical.

Although Bent at the time was planning to sell his fort to the government, Larkin failed to record anything concerning the matter. Only a few weeks before Larkin joined his wagon train, Bent had written a letter from Westport to the commandant of subsistence, Major George C. Waffman, at St. Louis indicating his desire and requesting that the many tons of government provisions stored at the fort be "removed or disposed of in some way."[13] Perhaps William Bent simply did not discuss his personal business activities with the wealthy traveller. Moreover, if government officials were somehow to hear of the whiskey incident, they might revoke Bent's licence to trade and be inclined to look less favorably on the purchase of the fort.

Nevertheless, while at Bent's New Fort, Larkin managed to record his experiences in some detail, leaving one of the best available descriptions of the fort and its daily affairs. On October 23 Larkin noted the presence of two unusual items used in the Indian trade: "Mr Bent got me to spin a humming top for him. He bro't out tops & Jumping Jacks for the Indians—they cost about ten cents each & he says he expects to get a robe a piece for them. . . ." Another of the most popular trade items was sugar, which was "more in demand among them than any other article. The[y] eat it raw just as small children would in the States. It costs them 50 c a cup or pound—coffee costing same."[14]

Larkin's poor health did not prevent him from participating in such diversions as were available at the remote frontier post. Although city-bred, Larkin was a skilled marksman whose abilities were proved when he won a shooting match with his Hawken rifle against five other men, Indian, Mexican, and Anglo. Also a sportsman, he hunted and fished alone or with Bent's employees. Despite the potential for trouble with the Indians, Larkin took an interest in the Cheyennes, Kiowas, and Arapahoes who hung about the fort. He spent several days observing their customs, as well as sampling some prickly pear fruit and attending a horse race.

From Bent's Fort To Santa Fe On October 26 a relieved Larkin departed Bent's New Fort, bound for Santa Fe. On the previous day Larkin had settled his account with Bent (he retained a credit of about twenty-two dollars), given a few presents to his host, and had his horse and two mules marked with Bent's brand. The party consisted of Larkin, with his own wagon and a "Mexican" driver, accompanied by five men and one wagon loaded with Bent's goods bound for Mora, New Mexico. The two wagons and seven men passed Bent's Old Fort on the twenty-eighth and Larkin briefly described in his diary the mouldering but not entirely abandoned post. After following Timpas Creek past the Three Buttes and on to the "Picketware" River, James was treated to one of the mountaineers' favorite delicacies, beaver tail. He wrote: "Some trappers came in & sold charley a lot of beaver tails, which are considered a great luxury among mountain men—they cost about 25 c each. We had one for dinner—boiled—it was surly [sic] delicious—somewhat as pigs feet should be."[15] Larkin's party on November 1 began the crossing of Raton Pass, the most arduous portion of the trip for wagons. After having repaired a broken wagon tongue and spring, Larkin's caravan completed the descent, and continued on toward the capital of the territory. He stayed at a "very polite & hospitable" Lucien Maxwell's hacienda on Rayado creek, where he met but regrettably failed to describe or even comment on the soon-to-be famous Kit Carson, whose first biography would appear in two years.[16]

Larkin's party proceeded to Mora, where he remained from November 7 to November 12. There he enjoyed a hospitable reception at the home of José Pley, where he met Ceran St. Vrain and William A. Bransford, two merchants engaged in the Santa Fe and Fort Union trades. He attended his first of many fandangos and committed to his diary a description of the "novel affair."[17] Also while at Mora Larkin heard from William Bransford that a Kiowa had been shot at Bent's Fort, an event he was grateful to have missed.

At Las Vegas Larkin was lodged and entertained at the house of the local padre, a Frenchman James failed to name, but who must have been Francisco Pinal (Jean François Pinard).[18] Getting underway once again, Larkin passed the famed pueblo and mission ruins at Pecos on November 14 and recorded his version of a tale noted by several writers concerning Montezuma and the perpetual fire at Pecos.[19] Just past the ruins the party arrived at "Jim Grey's house, a very comfortable place, where we enjoyed very good fare." The rancho was called Roseville, and was clearly a regular stopping place, but I have yet to find mention of it elsewhere.[20]

At last arriving at Santa Fe on November 15, Larkin

checked into the Fonda, or the Exchange Hotel, "the place of rendezvous for the better class of Americans."[21] Despite high prices for board and lodging at the hostelry, however, the accommodations at the Fonda proved unsatisfactory. The chimney in his room caught fire on the evening of December 21, and he was also disturbed by the sounds of gambling and boisterous guests in near proximity to his room.

Larkin was soon at home among the ranking military and mercantile society of Santa Fe, and he spent six weeks enjoying the new city and its diversions. He engaged in a variety of pleasant activities, including sightseeing, sleigh-riding, fandangos, and dinner parties. He witnessed a cock-fight, and he observed other native customs of Santa Fe. He also attended church at the old *parroquia,* and was invited to dine at Bishop Jean B. Lamy's residence north of Santa Fe. His Christmas in Santa Fe was tinged with homesickness compounded by an attack of dyspepsia, perhaps due to over-indulging in holiday fare. On December 30 James was offered a job as Paymaster's Clerk by Major Albert Smith, so he cancelled his plan for a return trip to St. Louis via San Antonio, Texas, and accepted the employment.

A Paymaster's Clerk In Santa Fe On December 31, 1856, Larkin inaugurated his brief career as a paymaster's clerk. With an escort of six soldiers, James and Major Smith left Santa Fe with the payroll for Fort Union, at which place they arrived on January 2. While there, James socialized with the officers, and after paying off the troops his party left Fort Union on January 5 for Santa Fe. His return to the territorial capital on January 8 coincided with a torchlight celebration commemorating the Battle of New Orleans. In the days that followed, Larkin found amusement in Santa Fe by attending military band concerts, debates, a court-martial, and numerous parties and social affairs.

Larkin's comments regarding "the present stupid race of Mexicans" are deeply etched with the prevailing ethnic biases of his time. The Missourian commented thus on the inhabitants of New Mexico: "The morals of the residents generally are very bad—the habits of the women are very loose, & the men addicted to gaming & stealing. . . . The Mexicans have a great passion for gambling, & will sometimes play off their last coat or blanket, so excited do they become." After observing a New Mexican funeral procession for a child, complete with a violin player and a cross-bearing youth, the uncomprehending diarist wrote: "These poor Mexicans seem rather like half civilized than otherwise."[22]

The diarist remained at Santa Fe until at least the beginning of March 1857, but the diary abruptly ends on January 31, 1857. By this time Larkin had sold his mules and ambulance to Thomas Bowler, "of Green & Bowler," and was making arrangements to settle his debt to Santa Fe trader James Josiah Webb. His diary indicates that he was preparing to return to St. Louis, but something occurred to change his plans. Research has not disclosed the reason for the change but it has revealed that James made not just one, but two trips across the plains in 1857.[23] Unfortunately, no record has appeared detailing Larkin's return trip in March to St. Louis, or his second prairie venture of 1857. However, it seems that Larkin decided to continue his prairie travels, and if his health was not fully restored, at least the trip seems not to have damaged the health-seeker. Letters written later in his life indicate that he remained for many years under the spell of the Santa Fe Trail, for he planned to make yet another trip to the plains in 1866. If he did so, however, no record has survived of a third trip.[24]

Part Two

Larkin's Santa Fe Trail Diary

[page 3]

Memorandum Book
of
Jas. R. Larkin
of St Louis Mo
Being on a trip from
St Louis to Bent's Fort
& other points in the
West.
September
1856

[page 10]

September 1856
Having returned home Sep 14th from a trip to Cape May,
Catskill Mts, Nahant, & Rockbridge Alum Springs &c[1] in

search of better health & not being permanently cured, I
find my mother & some of my friends desire me to go out
on the Plains of New Mexico. I accordingly visited Mr
Wm Bent,[2] a noted Indian Trader, & he consented that I
should go out in his train to his Fort—Known as Bent's
Fort—[3]situated on the Arkansas river, in the Western part
of the Territory of Kansas & near the N.W. boundary of
New Mexico—distant about 550[4] miles from Kansas City
&

[page 11]
100 [in ink, a later addition] miles from the base of the
Rocky Mts—Latitude 38° Longitude 36° about.
I made very hasty preparations for the trip as Mr Bent was
to start up from St Louis the next day after I first saw him,
& expected to be only a few days in Westport[5] the starting
point, so leaving me but few days to spare. Having been
kindly assisted by my mother [next five words inserted] &
Wm Glasgow[6], my cousin, in arranging for the trip. I left
St Louis on the Pacific R.R.[7] at 1 1/2 oclock P.M. 19th
inst., & arrived at Jeff. City 8 1/2 P.M. expecting to take
the "Morning Star"[8] same night—she however did not arrive until 20th about 11 oclock am & I then started on
her for Kansas. She also had my

[page 12]
carriage & other freight. Whilst waiting for the boat at
Jefferson City, I went to the Capitol & also to the Penitentiary[9] where I saw several familiar faces among the
prisoners—the two Wetmores confined for forgery in Land
Warrants, Wolf for do, & Robt Mc O'Blenis for murder.

The latter covered his face with his collar & hat & seemed disposed to be unknown—I did not speak to any of them. They were all confined & operating in the Coopers Shop.

The Missouri River is very low & the "M. Star" has much difficulty in getting up.

21st Sunday—Grounded last night & made but little progress arrived at Brunswick[10] in afternoon

[page 13]

& Miami about 8 oclock P.M.

22d Grounded again in night & run badly—arrived at Waverly[11] about 9 1/2 a.m. Saw a fine large flock of Pelicans.

I take to Kansas Gold	$250.00 per
"M. Star," & also about	200.00 in
pocket making total	$450.00

About 1 Oclock ran aground on Balbirnam Bar—sent passengers (gents) on a sand bar where they remained until near dark. Stage plank [?]. Got under way after dark & arrived at Lexington[12] about 12 oclock P.M.

23d Arrived at Kansas about 4 oclock P.M., left my goods there & went immediately out to Westport notwithstanding very disagreeable rumours of the ruffians or guerilla infesting the country. There is a set of miserable drunken creatures, who

[page 14]

hang about Westport & Kansas who certainly merit hanging but people do not put them down. Things are so disordered after the Kansas troubles.[13] I felt uneasy about

69

starting on my trip after hearing people talk as they did, but when I saw Mr Bent my fears seemed to dissipate as he appeared to apprehend no very bad trouble. Sept 25th I bot of Mr Hays[14] one pair of Mules costing $325.00— three years old—one of them rather poor, but will probably stand the trip. A horse I bot of H Clay Tate for $100.00—a very good animal for my trip being small, pony built—about 4 years old. My harness & saddle I also bot in Westport,

[page 15]
& almost all the balance of my outfit of Mess[rs.] Bernard.[15] After having mules shod in front & harness fitted on them, & getting my saddle, I am about ready for starting on my trip—which has hurried me very much from the time I concluded to go with Mr Bent. After dinner we made a start to go out to camp where the wagons were stationed distant about 3 miles. Mr Bent had assigned a Mr Hamilton[16] to drive my waggon out there, but as the gent indulged too freely in drinking with his parting friends, we were on the point of leaving him, when he returned able to walk pretty straight—so I allowed him to drive. A short distance out from Kansas we crossed the Border Line of Missouri, to which state I bid "Farewell," & then entered the Territory of Kansas. Arrived at camp about 3 oclock, waited for a pair of Mules

[page 16]
which Mr Bent bot & also some apples for our mess. We finally got under way & after a slow travel arrived at Indian Creek[17] where we camped for the night—my first experience. We had a good supper of very fine sweet potatoes

fresh pork, bread & coffee. We came across a very good
man there—Jim Young, who was very highly recommended by Mr Bent, & he engaged him for me at the
rate of Twenty Five Dollars $25.00 per Month—he to
drive my carriage, take care of mules & horse & to make
himself generally useful—I am very much pleased with
him—he went to work almost immediately after being engaged at cooking for our mess. He was formerly a sailor,
but gave up the life & came from Balto [Baltimore] out to

[page 17]

the plains where he has been for past year almost.
Sept 26th Started early in the morning, without breakfasting and travelled until about 11 oclock, when we breakfasted & dined, made a halt of 2 1/2 hours, & travelled to
Bulls' Creek[18] making about 20 miles today. In evening we
were joined by Mr Allison's[19] train from Independence—
Going to Walnut Creek—[20] he joined us for safety—
fearing the Yankees would give him trouble.
Sep 27th Early in the morning, I found my horse was
missing—Mr Bent sent a number of men after him—but
they did not find him. One reported finding his tracks
going towards Westport. After waiting for sometime we
started on without him, leaving an Indian to hunt him &
bring him up to our camp.

[page 18]

We travelled today as far as Willow Creek or Spring—[21]
about 20 miles, where we camped—found some new wa-
termellons & sweet milk for our coffee quite a treat. Today
we passed in sight of Lawrence[22] & are now within about
12 miles of it. Within past 2 days we have passed houses

uninhabited on account of the Kansas difficulties, & some that have been burned. One was burning as we passed. Almost every one living on the road has been plundered, robbed or driven away by one side or the other— Missourians or Freesoilers. The country is in an awful con- dition at present, no one knowing how long his house, goods or stock may be safe from the maurauders. A heavy rain came up after supper but I was dry in my carriage.

[page 19]
Sep 28th Started after breakfasting & travelled as far as Hundred & Ten—[23] a rather troublesome place—having been headquarters of some of the ruffians in the country. We felt more apprehension of trouble here, than back of it, but had no difficulty—some of Allisons mules ran off at night, but after a run were secured next day. Weather quite cold & disagreeable.
Sep 29th Left 110 & travelled to Soldier Creek[24] about 18 miles—not making a very long trip as the animals needed water & grass, both good here. Very cold & windy—quite cold enough for snow—Took my first ride on horseback today on Mr Hamiltons Horse—rode about 8 miles rather cool work—but warmer than in the carriage.
Wrote to J & WR Bernard & H C Tate about my horse & also wrote home to my mother—by the Council Grove mail.

[page 20]
Today passed thro' Prairie City—[25] a Yankee city—they have a steam saw-mill & a liberty pole & about 3 houses in the place. Country around is beautiful. In our train we have quite a number of nations represented—Americans,

Mexicans, French, Germans & Pawnee Indians—
numbering about 16 men. We have also Mr Bents Lady,[26]
an Indian woman—the "old Scwaw" as he calls her, &
also her pet—a little Pawnee Indian, who was a prisoner,
among the [blank in ms.] Indians, & bot by Mr Bent. He
is a great favorite with the old lady. Charley—our waggon-
master is a very gentlemanly—clean man. Old Klaber—a
German—very sociable & loquacious—is a great
addition—having always a word to say. His favorite theme
seems to be about Buaffalos. He & I have conversations in
German—rather broken on both sides, as he is not

[page 21]

a very perfect scholar.
Sep 30th Slept rather cool last night had cold feet—did
not bundle up enough. At noon we stopped near 142—[27]
the man who formerly lived there had been robbed, his
store entered by 11 men & his goods taken—he had left
for the grove. Work of Abolitionists I expect.
Nothing of much interest today, Camped on Bluff Creek
& made about 28 miles.
October 1st Started early in the morning leaving Allisons
train behind as he had lost some mules, passed Rock
Creek, where I was so foolish as to miss a good warm
breakfast in a stone house, a chance I'll not likely let pass
again. Nooned at Council Grove[28] & bought what few articles we needed. I bought 6 Bus. Corn there at $1.50 per
Bus. $10.00 a good price.

[page 22]

I endeavored to get a good horse, but did not succeed.
The Kaw[29] Indians live here & in the neighborhood—a

73

number of them paid us a visit, & as they laid around our carriages, well merited their names as Kaws—from the noises they made in conversing. Starting up again we travelled to Elm Creek & camped, making about 20 miles. Weather has moderated & is now quite warm & genial— the wind & dust on the road however is very disagreeable. Oct 2nd Making a start early travelled to Diamond Spring Creek[30] about 11 miles—expecting one of Majors & Russells[31] trains & one that belonged to Dr H Connelly.[32] There is a house

[page 23]

near D Spring & also a carrell—a stone fence to keep stock in limits, built by Santa Fe Mail Co.[33] I shot a grouse the first game killed on the trip, except a pig in the troubled districts. Mr B shot at a wolf on the prairies, but missed him. Camped at Lost Creek, running thru the Prairies, having no trees bordering on it—made 23 miles about. Left a letter for my mother yesterday at Council Grove to go in next mail. Paid Jas. Young Twenty [previous word crossed out in ms.] Ten Dollars $10.00 on a/c. Oct 3rd Travelled along finely & near night camped at Cottonwood—[34] before reaching here, we met the young Kings of Georgia,[35] who went out with Mr B in June & have been at the Fort & Soda Spring[36] & neighborhood since. They were returning to the States & camped with

[page 24]

us. They are very fine young men, who went out in bad health & are now returning fat & hearty. They bro't a letter to Mr B informing him of some difficulty or trouble at his fort, & caused him to conclude to start posthaste

74

thither. Accordingly we started same night from camp
with our two carriages & one provision waggon drawn by
four mules leaving the train to come on after. Grand Celebration.
Oct 4th Saturday—Drove very hard & nooned about 2
oclock at Little Arkansas river—[37] a very small stream at
present—2 feet wide in some places. We saw an immense
number of Buffalos today for the first time—they look like
huge masses of indian rubber

[page 25]
bouncing along the prairies—raising no little dust. Mr
Bent went out from Camp at noon—about 2000 yards &
shot three—one calf, one cow & one young Bull, I got
one shot at the Bull & Mr B says I hit him, but he managed to bound off. The cow meat had hardly got cold before it was on our fire cooking for dinner. (Cows are the
choice meat, old Bulls not considered very palatable) I
saw 5 antelopes in one herd this morning, & also saw a
number of wolves. There are a great many small birds on
the prairies—I dont know what kind however. It's very
exciting sport to see a great herd of Buffalo running across
your path ahead, or grazing on the plains, & creep &
crawl up

[page 26]
to get a shot at them. Today [crossed out] I felt better from
the excitement. (I have been very costive for several days,
& today had a tremendous passage & am much
improved [)] It seems persons frequently become costive in
starting across, but I felt no great inconvenience from it as
I would have felt at home. Started after dinner & trav-

elled about 10 Miles, being within about 3 miles of Where
Chaves was murdered some years since—[38] Have made today about fifty miles, including our night travel—expect
to reach the fort in 7 or 8 days if our animals hold out
well. The wolves howling & crying near our camp makes a
hideous noise.
Oct 5th Sunday Made an early start & went to Cow
Creek[39] for

[page 27]
breakfast. Cow Creek is quite a prominent stream, some
parts of it being quite wide & deep. I hunted about it for
game but did not kill anything. Old Klaber an interesting
old German, who drives our provision wagon, got into the
mud with his wagon & had to take out most of his load.
Travelled slowly today—the weather being very warm—
thermometer 89 ° & part of the road sandy & heavy, the
horses could not make much progress—the small mus-
quitos [crossed out in ms.] buffalo knats troubling them
very much. About 4 oclock we reached the Arkansas
river,[40] where we camped at a pretty spot for bathing. I
took advantage of it & took a good bath, after which was
quite refreshed. The stream is very low many sandbars
being in sight. About 7 oclock we reached Walnut
Creek[41] where there is a rude trading store kept by Booth
& Allison.[42] A hard looking set

[page 28]
of men were staying there for what reason, we do not
know—were quite inquisitive about where our camping
place would be & did not know but they designed stealing
our mules, which they very much admired, but were not

troubled with them. Hearing there was a camp of Cheyenne Indians[43] a short distance off, we approached their
camp & sent a mexican to inform them Mr Bent wished
to see them. They soon came charging up to our camp on
their ponies, making quite a hubbub. Down they seated
themselves in a circle & had a long talk until Mr B treated
them to coffee & bread, which they eat heartily. They
presented quite a warlike appearance, being young Cheyenne warriors in one War Party against the Pawnees—
almost all were armed, some

[page 29]
with muskets or guns & others with their own [last two
word crossed out in ms.] implements of their own make.
Some of them rested their guns on my carriage wheel,
which I did not much fancy—being in it, but the old
squaw spied the danger & made them move them. They
wear their hair long reaching near their waists, & parted
in the center like the women—when they are in mourn-
ing they cut off one side. They were very sociable to us—
Mr B. being a great favorite of the tribe & his squaw being
of the same. They had a very pleasant time chatting with
Mr B & the old squaw, & seemed very much pleased. To
meet them with any other man than Mr Bent—might not
be to agreeable—they being rather on the savage order.
Mr. B. informed them of the report that reached Sts.
[states] before we started, that a number of their tribe

[page 30]
had been killed & taken prisoner at or near Fort Laramie
by the U.S. Troops, but they had not or pretended not to
have heard of it, & looked quite serious on learning it.[44]

We made 25 miles today—I left them [word crossed out in ms.] some of them there talking with Mr B's Lady when I went to bed—not very well understanding their language. Oct 6th Monday. Soon after starting we met a number more of Cheyennes, ferocious looking fellows, some of them, & rather handsomely dressed—had to give them some sugar & coffee & off they went. We were joined by two Cheyennes who intend going the most of the way on with us—they have rather poor horses & will probably break them down. Yesterday eve saw an immense number of buffalo—some of them very gentle, & Mr B & myself had a number of shots at them—grand sport.

[page 31]
the excitement hunting them is very exhilarating—I enjoyed it very much. We had load enough in our waggon & did not do them any serious injury—altho' I tho't I made one jump as if hurt. They should be hit just near the [previous two words crossed out in ms.] behind the foreleg—near the heart. The old Bulls are very ferocious, & when wounded are very dangerous, as they fight furiously. Wolves—white & grey—ranging about the prairies in plenty. After starting on the Ridge Road or Dry Road (of the Arkansas) being a cut off by which some 12 miles are saved, instead of taking the River Route, we camped near a hole of muddy water—unfit for use. Oct—Mr B. in a very good communicative humor—Old Scquaw

[page 32]
& his doings. Rather funny.
Oct 7th After a long trip & hunting of [previous two

words crossed out in ms.] without water we finally found some passably good, & halted for breakfast at 2 1/2 oclock—rather late even for lazy people. Started on & reached Arkansas about 6 1/2 o'clock in evening & right glad to see it—the water being very good. Two trains passed down last night & one this morning.

Oct 8th Started early and travelled a short distance to near Fort Atkinson, or Fort Mackay—[45] while camping a number of Kioway Indians came into camp & had a talk. We passed the village [written over word "camp," crossed out in ms.] at Fort Atkinson (an old fort now abandoned & in ruins) consisting of a large number of

[page 33]

lodges (circular tents covered with canvass or skins of animals & supported by a number of poles tied at the top— they have an opening at the bottom for the Indians to crawl in, & one at the top for the smoke to escape). The most of the men now out hunting & did not see many of them—Saw a number of boys almost naked—with the largest bellies I ever saw on such sized children—they really looked deformed. There was a tremendous lot of horses ranging near their camp some of them very beautiful—These Indians are about the worst set in this part of the country—being treacherous & deceitful—but they suffered us to pass unmolested. We camped at noon below the Crossing of the Arkansas,[46] & met one of Major

[page 34]

& Russells trains, by which I sent a letter to my brother Hilles.[47] Saw but little game today & not much of interest occurred. I am not very well—having eaten some thing that disagreed with me. For several nights past have had heavy strong winds—Similar to those on the ocean. One of our Cheyenne Indians has a novel set of shoes for his horse consisting of Buffalo skin—cut in round pieces about 8 in[ches] diameter—he ties them on with strings— the leather being placed over the bottom of the foot & tied around the leg.

Oct 9th After travelling a good distance camped near the Arkansas—there being a storm coming up—Had hardly got settled down before on it came, raining & blowing a gale—during the night

[page 35]

the thunder & lightning was tremendous—I was quite un- easy in my wagon with so much iron—my guns, pistols, powder &c, but was not struck—altho' much exposed on a hill. The rain beat very hard against my carriage, & completely drenched my driver, sleeping under it, but I kept quite warm.

Oct 10th weather changed—much cooler & rain still con- tinues—Old Klaber came begging for a drink, & as he & the rest needed it, being exposed to the weather, I open [previous word crossed out in ms.] had a bottle of my fine brandy brought out, for I [previous two words crossed out in ms.] which was speedily consumed. We made but little progress today, roads being very muddy & heavy—about 20 miles & reached Chouteau's Island[48] in evening which is about 80 miles from Bents Fort. It was so damp & wet, I did not get out on the ground at all today, but remained housed up in my carriage.

Oct 11th Saturday Rain—Rain—Rain.

[page 36]

Oct 12th Sunday Weather cold & damp. We travelled very hard today—the roads very muddy & heavy—the animals did not make much speed. Mr Bent being anxious to get on to the Fort, pushed ahead at any rate. In the night we started out again & made a few miles.

Monday Oct 13th Urging our mules on we arrived at the Fort in the morning about 10 o'clock. Bent's Fort[49] is situated on the north side of the Arkansas River on a bold bluff—being very accessible however from the North Side. It is built of brown sandstone—being about 170 feet long & 80 feet wide. The walls are about 14 [added in ink at a later time] feet high, & the houses are ranged around the inside

[page 37]

next to the walls—leaving a large open space in center. There are 15 rooms, being used for sleeping rooms, store rooms, dining room & kitchen & one lookout tower on top [previous six words added at a later time]. The Fort faces East & the entrance is surmounted with a large pair of antlers—It is used by Mr Wm Bent as a trading post with the Indians—the Cheyennes, Kioways, Arrapahoes & Comanches ranging in the neighborhood—they bring their Buffalo Robes, Tongues & Dried Buffalo Meat, Antelope & Deer skins to him & take in exchange Coffee, Sugar, Powder, Flour & Balls—on which a large profit is made. Sugar seems to be more in demand amongst them than any other article—The[y] eat it raw just as small children would in the States—It costs them 50 c a cup or pound—coffee costing same.

[page 38]

Any thing of value is said to be worth "so many robes."
The Cheyennes are great friends of Mr. B. Arrapahoes &
Comanches are also friendly—Kioways rather so. These
latter Indians are great rascals & very unreliable.
When we approached the Fort there was a number of
Cheyenne and Kioway Lodges—stationed near by. The
news rec'd from the Indians was very unfavorable—the
Cheyennes having Killed 14 whites & done [previous
word crossed out in ms.] committed other depredations—
so their people report of some of their tribe ranging farther
north than this. The Indian principle is—if any of their
men are killed to kill any white man in return—whether
he is the murderer or not. Some of their tribe had been
killed at or near Fort Kearney[50] by the U. G. [United
States Government] Troops, who will

[page 39]

[following two sentences added later in brown ink] Memo.
I left in Mr. W.W. Bents charge & keeping—one money
belt—containing $230.00 Gold Kept about $53.00 in
Pocket Book
be very apt to extend their operations further. We need
however not apprehend much danger, as they are friendly
with Mr Bent.
I was rather homesick & gloomy after arriving here—not
fancying the state of affairs, mode of living, condition of
society &c, but as I could not well better it, I managed to
keep in a tolerable humour. I certainly could have gotten
along about as well in Virginia as here, & my health perhaps equally as much benefitted, without the trouble &
expense of such a trip in the wilderness. The fare is very

plain—being generally Dried Buffalo Meat boiled with
Mexican corn, Coffee, Sugar, Biscuit & Butter—nothing
very dangerous in that for dyspeptics.

The manner of living among the Squaws is rather looser
than civil-

[page 40]

ized people generally permit. We found affairs at the Fort
had been in much confusion—Mr Bent left a Frenchman
to do the trading with the Indians, & a young man named
Vogle[51] from Westport to keep the books. The Frenchman
had been giving the Indians Whiskey, thereby running Mr
B. in danger of losing his license that being strictly forbid-
den by U.S. laws. His management had not been proper—& gave Mr B. much dissatisfaction. Several of the
Indians had been drunk & carrying very [previous word
crossed out in ms.] on badly. Mr B. resolved to discharge
him & let him go his way, which he did on Tuesday
14th Oct. One of the Kioways who was a great friend of
the Frenchman, (he had given him liquor)

[page 41]

was much displeased thereby & in the evening came into
the Fort & blamed Mr B. for sending the man off. Mr B.
became very much enraged at him, as he had also been at
the Fren[chman] & abused the man & his race (Kioways)
prodigiously. The Kiowah—named Pawnee was one of
their chiefs, draws his knife on Mr B., who grasped out
[previous word crossed out in ms.] his pistol & might instantly have shot him had it not been for the interference
of some Cheyennes, who were witness to the transaction.

Many angry words passed, in by no means a peaceable manner, & Mr Bent struck the Frenchman one or two blows & drove him out of the Fort, giving him a kick before his Kioway friend, & accompanying it with an insulting remark. Instantly the Cheyennes became

[page 42]
uneasy & alarmed—they being on our side & unfriendly to the Kioways & fearing an attack. Their women & children came running in the Fort—the former bearing their large packs on their backs, & the men also remained inside during the night to assist in case of an attack from the hostile band. Arms were gotten out hurridly examined & loaded, & with all the hurry & clamour—the scene was truly on the warlike order—such as I never before had witnessed. Our horses were all driven inside of the fort for safety, as the K's might have killed them or driven them away. I became sli [previous two words crossed out in ms.] was not much alarmed for our safety, as we had a strong fort, plenty of arms & ammunition, about 20 Mexicans & 20 Cheyennes to defend us. The state of affairs however did not well suit me, and I remained up for

[page 43]
some time during the night. I could hear the drums beating outside—a signal for an attack. The Frenchman had probably been talking to some of the K's, & inducing them to take his part. Mr B. felt very independent as to their friendship, as he is head captain of one of the C's [Cheyennes] bands of soldiers, & could easily set them against the K's [Kiowas]—the C's being the most nu-

merous however would overpower them. They are both a
brave & fighting set of men. Mr B. says he will start the
war against them—in that case it will not be very pleasant
here, & unsafe to go far outside hunting, & I will probably
leave in time for Santa Fé, where I hope to be more satisfied at any rate than here. The weather today was much
more pleasant than for some time past & I

[page 44]

was more satisfied with matters on a bright sunshiny day.
Oct 15th. Warm & pleasant. No attack occurred last
night & we rested tolerably well. Very few Kioways came
inside today—one old man paid us a visit—but rec'd cold
treatment & left. A messenger has gone after some of the
Cheyenne warriors, who will soon come to our aid. I did
not go far outside not deeming it very prudent.
A number of Cheyennes [previous word crossed out in
ms.] Arrapahoes came in today, & their women packed
out a number of the tent covers—carrying great loads—
the poor women have to do all the work, & are great
drudges—they can carry very heavy burdens on their
backs—having them fastened on by a strap passed over
their shoulders & around their necks. They do not enjoy a
very good name—for some reason—

[page 45]

It is interesting to see the Indians travelling—they fasten
one end of their lodge poles on the horse, let the other
drag on the ground, & put their children in a kind of large
Basket fastened to the poles.
Oct 16th Mr Bent gave the Arrapahoe visitors a feast

today—they call any thing a feast in the way of a dinner.
Times rather dull.

Oct 17th I started out hunting this morning & rode about
10 miles, but only saw two turkeys—game seeming to be
very scarce—as there are so many Indians in the neighborhood. I was accompanied by Mr Bent's Mexico Indian
Hunter. Came back quite fatigued. We crossed the Arkansas, & went up on [the] other side & recrossed about 4
miles above & passed a Comanche camp, & also passed a
large Arrapahoe village or camp.

[page 46]

The women were engaged in preparing their robes, hung
on scaffolds.

Oct 18th Saturday. I went fishing in the morning near the
fort, but caught only one small fish. Poor Sport. In afternoon took my rifle and shot at a mark. In evening felt
quite unwell having eaten something that disagreed with
me. I was visited today by several young Sqwaws—two of
whom came to make me a present of two plates of cactus
or Prickly Pear Apples[.] The finest looking Squaw presented them—but few speeches were made on the occasion, as we could not well understand each other. The
fruit is much eaten by the Indians—It looks somewhat
like a short pepperpod—being reddish & of near the same
shape. The taste resembles that of quince preserves. A few
Apaches came into the fort today.

[page 47]

Several young Cheyenne warriors returned today from a
war-party against the Pawnees—They report having killed

86

one Pawnee. Their appearance was not very prepossessing as some of them had their faces blacked up in a disagreeable manner. After their return, some of the other cheyennes here—also had their faces blacked—a custom of theirs after having killed an enemy—If they lose a man they cut off part of their hair.

Oct 19th Sunday Weather warm & delightful as spring. After reading for some time in morning, I took a walk up above the Fort, near where the Arrapahoes had been camping. When there I was called by an old chief to come to him, which I did & found it to be old Pawnee—the Kiowah chief with whom Mr Bent had quarrelled. He made signs & spoke to me & seemed

[page 48]

to signify that he was going to fight the Americans & Cheyennes. I had Harpers [magazine] for September[52] with me, containing a number of cuts, or engravings—of Indians &c. I should [previous word crossed out in ms.] showed them to the old man, & the Squaw & a lot of children soon gathered around to take a look at such a novelty—They were very much pleased with the sights. The Indians are not very neat in their toilet—when I was sitting there on their blanket, the old squaw commenced making researches on the cranium of one of the children for some hidden object. I know not if she was successful— I left after that. Lent old Klaber my gun & he returned with a fine duck—quite a treat for dinner. I eat perhaps too much, as I was quite unwell after it. I do not think the air here agrees with me as well as mountain air of Virginia.

[page 49]

The Arrapahoes had a horse race today—they ran a number of races distance short—but great speed. The sport
was quite exciting. There was also a foot race near the
fort. In the evening the cheyennes got up a dance—
Music—a sort of drum (sounding like beating on a dry
goods box) and their disagreeable *yahying* & singing. Considerable celebration for Sunday. The day is kept as a day
of rest in the fort.

Oct 20th. In the morning I tried a mare that Mr Bent
wished to sell me & like her tolerably well.

Oct 21st Hamilton & [Dave?]—arrived today from the
train—which they report a short distance off. Oct 22d
The train arrived early in the morning—[53] the cattle were
much worn out. There was quite a

[page 50]

stir in Fort getting out the goods & putting them away.
I eat a little molasses, & suffered for it afterwards—it does
not seem to agree with me.

Oct 23d Gloomy & cloudy—misty in morning & rain &
sleet in afternoon. The day passed off very rapidly. I was
engaged in the morning writing home to my friends. Mr
Bent got me to spin a humming top for him. He bro't out
tops & Jumping Jacks for the Indians—they cost about ten
cents each & he says he expects to get a Robe a piece for
them—Robes are worth about Seven Dollars in St
Louis—Quite a pretty profit.[54]

Oct 23d [23d written over 24th in ms.] Not much doing
today. There is an old Indian here who has an arm that
was broken four times in the same place, he had it attended

[page 51]
to twice, & finally let it go as it would & it is now hanging by the skin & flesh & seems to be well. He can twist
& turn it almost as he pleases—it is almost unpleasant to
see him work it about—especially as it causes him no
pain. Quite a curiosity.
24th [24th written over 25th in ms.] Mr Bent decided today to send two waggons over to Moro to take some goods
of his own & mine, & as I am not sufficiently benefitted
here by the air, & not pleased with matters as they are, &
prospects of Indian difficulties ahead, I am greatly pleased
with the arrangements. I am anxious to get to New Mexico & this is about the only safe opportunity for me to
go—as there is danger of attack by the Indians if I only
had one or two men. I bought a mare of Mr B. today for
$75.00—a good animal

[page 52]
about six years old & very gentle.
Had a shooting party in the afternoon—I had the honor
of being the best shot at the longest distance about 275
yards with rifle, & third best at short distance. There were
six marksmen, white, Indian & Mexican.[55]
25th Saturday. [25th written over 26th in ms.] As I am
going to start to-morrow with the train, I have been very
busily engaged making preparations for the trip. Have had
my two mules branded—one WB [linked as a single unit]
one WB [WB upside-down] & my horse WB—being Mr
Wm W Bents mark.[56] Have made Mr Bent a present of
molasses, White Fish, & Pickles. I am to have credit on
Mr Bents Books for 1 Bbl Apples $3.00, Bottle Quinine to
Hamilton $5.00, & money lent to Mr B $10.00 & $3.00

for Powder for John & also $1.25 for Powder Horn for
John.
Have had my harness oiled up, & en-

[page 53]
gaged a Mexican to go over with me to assist taking care
horses &c. Pay $12.00 per Month.
26th Sunday After having all ready for the trip we made a
start for Moro, New Mexico—having two wagons cont'g
goods belonging to Mr Bent in one, & my goods in the
other (provisions &c.)—we have seven in our party, 3
[over 4 in ms.] Mexicans 4 Americans. Not starting till
late about 12 oclock, we only made about 10 Miles.
27th Monday Our cattle strayed away last night & went
within about 3 miles of the Fort & we were detained until
about 10 oclock before starting.
I find the mare I bot of Mr Bent has some sickness—a
heaving of the breast, blowing & a swelling under the
mouth. As I wanted a horse very much I have kept her &
run the risk of any thing worse

[page 54]
We are accompanied by old Hazyatooya a great friend of
the whites, his squaw & several others—they hang on to
get the meals—I let them fall to, after we finish. Today we
come in sight of the GreenHorn Mountain[57] covered with
Snow—they are about 100 [100 written over 200 in ms.]
Miles distant, & look beautiful in the sunshine. We made
about 12 miles & encamped near Purgatory River.[58] The
day has been delightful—altho' there was a very heavy
frost.

Several Mexican Indians [previous three words crossed out in ms.] One Mexican & one Indian came to camp today & report snow in mountains.

28th Tuesday. In the morning we met Mr Jno [John] Smith (an old Cheyenne Interpreter)[59] & his friend—going to Bents Fort—they stopped & took breakfast. We travelled about 20 miles today—passing Bent's Old Fort[60] (now in ruins, having been

[page 55]

set on fire several times. It was once quite an imposing fort built of adobe, but is now much dilapidated.[)]
[the following was inserted at top of page:] 28th Weather very cool in morning ther[mometer] 32 ° at 2 oclock abt 70°. a number of Mexicans were camping there. We crossed the Arkansas near the Fort, & travelled up as far as the Rio Timpas [previous six words crossed out in ms.] about 8 miles on the Arkansas where we camped & prepared for a long march of 20 miles tomorrow—this a dry sterile country—getting plenty of wood & water. We are today in sight of the Wahtahyah[61] & Green Horn Mts.—snowy capped.

29th Oct Wednesday. Started about 3 a.m. & travelled about 14 miles & camped for breakfast at 8 a.m. travelling towards the Timpas.[62] The country is very sterile being almost bare of any thing but clumps of grass & cactus. We found a little water here—rather unusual. A wolf paid my mare a visit last night & bit off the lariett (for the grease that was on it)—the mare being gentle did not leave. We today passed the "3 Buttes"[63] of Irregular appearance, composed of limestone & earth.

[page 56]

They present an imposing appearance looming up their lofty heads. The country is now gradually ascending as we go towards the Rocky Mts. We travelled until about 4 oclock reaching the Timpas, a small stream with steep banks—found some pools of water & luxuriant grass. Made about 13 miles—total today about 27 miles—a very good trip.

Weather cool in morning & quite warm at midday. The country we pass thro' today is somewhat like a desert with a scattered growth of grass. Heavy clouds in evening made me fear a storm, but fortunately it passed over.

30th Oct. Thursday Travelled as far as the crossing of the Timpas[64] & nooned. We saw the immense tracks of a grizzly bear & one of the Mexicans got a view of his lordship & was on the point of firing when Bruin heard the cracks of whips & ran away—Lucky—for they are dangerous.

[page 57]

We met 3 Mexicans walking from Taos They report having seen the bears tracks—no snow in the Raton Mts & the Eutaws & Apaches (Indians much to be dreaded on our route) at peace.

There occurred a squabble between charley the Waggon Master & myself—but soon over. Travelled after nooning to "Hole in the Rock"[65] & camped—found very good water. Saw plenty of antelope this afternoon for the first time. We yesterday used the Grease Bush for fire, it burns excellently—today we have an abundance of cedar, burning beautifully & emitting an odor not unpleasant.

31st Oct Friday. Travelled to "Hole in the Prairie"[66] &

nooned—saw plenty of antelopes. From there went as far as Purgatory River (or Picketware of mountain men) making about 27 miles. The P. is a clear running mountain stream, where we camped, but is said to

[page 58]
disappear below, running into the ground. We camped in the bushes after crossing & found almost no grass at all. Today the Wahtahyah & Pikes Peak,[67] and a chain of the Rocky Mts in view—looming up towards the heavens. In the night charley, Filippe (a jolly little Mexican) Paul & myself started out turkey hunting—as they abound here. We had a Mexican along who went ahead, & finding where the turkeys were roosting, built great fires under the trees, so as to dazzle & blind them. At the first tree I killed two, at the second one, & returning shot one on first tree again—Charley shot three making total after a short hunt for 7 turkeys.[68] The brush was very thick & hard to get thro', but the sport was great; the[y] came tumbling down with great force & fat as need ever be. They are a treat, as we are out of fresh meat. The strange Mexican—crossed us over the Purgatory on his back—being stripped to the shirt, but did not seem to mind it.

[page 59]
November 1st Saturday. Started about daylight & travelled up the valley of the Purgatory about 8 miles, & finding good grass, stopped to noon. We are now on the point of starting up the Raton Mts—a ragged looking chain of Mts—that strikes the Purgatory at right angles & divides the waters of the Arkansas from those of the Canadian.

We have now got into the Piñon or pine neighborhood—
it burns beautifully & bears a resinous nut eaten by Mexicans & Indians & is very palatable. It is said that fruit fails
here in the mountains every other season, & we have now
a chance for Pinons &c, as last year was unfavorable. Had
a good run after a drove of turkeys after getting to camp.
Some trappers came in & sold charley a lot of beaver tails,
which are considered a great luxury among mountain
men—they cost about 25 c each. We had one for dinner—boiled—it was surly delicious—somewhat as pigs
feet should be.

[page 60]
Where we are camped is a delightful spot—the weather
being now charming—the air here is lovely—a delicious
breeze fanning us all the time. Hearing reports of dryness
in the mountains we remained here until about 3 1/2
P.M. & then started to make a short trip to grass in the
mountains. Started on & saw many deer on the hills, but
shot none. No bears (grizzley) in sight altho' their
footprints are numerous. Met a Mexican boy on a fine
horse, without saddle or bridle. He inquired the way to
Arkansas & said he was hunting water & that there were
people coming behind. We camped at a very pretty spot &
soon after stopping—the Mexican boy came back, & we
let him pass. After he had gotten away, we feared he
might be a spy of some of the Eutaws or Apache [previous
two words crossed out in ms.] Indians. I had my horse &
mules picketed & hobbled & was not entirely contented
with prospects as the Indians, had there been any, could
easily have overcome us here.

[page 61]

Our fears were groundless however as the fellow was afterwards caught—& proved to have stolen the horse—he
was sent to Taos.

Sunday Nov 2d Started early & soon had a snow storm—
which was by no means agreeable, spoiling our hunting &
the view of the scenery among the Mts. Made very good
progress today climbing hill after hill until we finally
reached the summit that we cross—here the wind was se-
verely cold & snow came down bravely. The scenery ascending the Mt. is beautiful. From the summit there is a
fine view of the Wattahyah, Pikes Peak & the chain running South from the Wattahyah.

The descent is much more sudden than the ascent, & the
most difficult & troublesome part of the road. Camped in
the evening in the snow, but soon made a cheerful blazing
fire that warmed us up & after a good night rest again
commenced descending on [following word is illegible in
ms.]

[page 62]

3d Nov Monday. Today we met with some trouble—on ascending a hill one of our wagon tongues broke, but fortunately soon was mended—but in passing over an
extremely rocky & rough road I had one of the springs of
my wagon broken—that soon however was fastened up
again with a pair of old larrietts, & we pushed ahead. My
waggon was let down the worst hill by hand, there being
danger of braking the tongue, if the mules should have
slipped & fallen on the slippery snow. We all reached the
bottom of the last hill in safety, & felt much rejoiced.
Some of the hills are awful for waggons or carriages as they

are very steep, & some of them almost nothing but rocks. After [previous word crossed out in ms.] The Raton may be called the dread of all mountain travellers in this coun-try but the road could be made a good one with the ex-penditure of $25,000.00[69]

[page 63]

After camping & taking a meal, we again pushed on & reached the Rio Canadiano—or Canadian[70] & camped for the night.

4th Nov Tuesday Last night was very cold & disagreeable, but after 11 oclock today the weather moderated & be-came very pleasant. Travelled today about 24 miles to the Vermejo [written with a *j* over an *h* in original ms.] River,[71] a swift running stream from the Mts. & camped on the other side. As I rode during the snow storm almost all day before yesterday, I am again attacked with rheuma-tism in my right arm—as I had at home, but not so se-verely.

5th Nov Wednesday Travelled to the Cimmeron & nooned. Here we found some traces of civilization, some adobe or mud cabins, occupied by a few Mexicans, em-ployed by Mr Maxwell of Rial [Rayado] We obtained some fresh eggs & Mexican cheese here & had a fine breakfast of venison, eggs, cheese & molasses, of which I ate rather too heartily.[72]

[page 64]

We met Kit Carson[73] here—he was on his way hunting, accompanied by a number of men. We were passed here by

a set of hunters returning from a hunt—They had a large
quantity of venison &c packed on mules—some of the
mules looked as if a few pounds more would stop them.
An old man on a very small mule excited much merriment
by his appearance & that of his mule. We started on &
travelled to Rial,[74] a small place owned by Mr Maxwell
who married a Mexican woman of wealth, & owns large
droves of cattle hereabouts. We remained here for the
night & until about 12 oclock next day
Nov 6th Thursday
when we pushed ahead about 6 miles. Mr M. was very polite & hospitable. There is quite a large gap in the mountains, but a short distance from Rial & a tremendous wind
blew down thro' the place. Proceeded as far as about 8
miles from ocate & camped the day having been very disagreeable & windy.
Nov 7th Friday. Started early in the

[page 65]
morning. Passed the ocate [creek] & camped in a sheltered
place in the valley. A snow storm came on in the morning, when the weather was very cold. I started after nooning in my carriage with charley the waggon-master &
travelled to Moro,[75] which place we reached about dusk
in the evening, after a very hard drive for the mules—
they having made about 42 miles. I found Col St Vrain[76]
at Mr Jos Play's[77] house, and was very kindly & hospitably
rec'd. I lodged in Mr. Play's house, there being no hotel of
any worth in Moro—his accommodations are very fine—
he has an old Negro cook from New Orleans, who fills her
place well. Moro is a small place, situated on Moro River,
built of adobe houses, & presents a poor aspect. I met here

97

Mr W. A. Bransford,[78] a merchant of this place, who has sold out to Mr Play.
Nov 8th Saturday. Col. St Vrain left for Fort Union. The train arrived with my goods. Charley calls the weight of my goods 1100# to Moro frt [freight] to be six cents.[per pound]

[page 66]
Went to a fandango this evening—a novel affair—every one almost was there. The Mexicans dance very grace-fully—They are smoking almost all the time. Had a bar-room attached to the large dansing room, where much liquor was drank, & a Monte Bank attended by a woman was in full operation. A gent asks any lady to dance—their principal figure seemed to be a mixture of a waltz & baluner[?] The smoking was so great that I got sleepy & retired.[79] The music consisted of a couple of fiddles, & I believe a guitar—& also one of the musicians singing with the music. Nov 9th Sunday. I started in the morning with a Mr Fisher to go trout fishing up to Awa Negro, Black Water, a mountain stream about 7 miles off, but caught no fish, & got a little wet. Eat some Mexican Molasses, made from cornstalk, & some cheese. The Molasses disagreed with me & I felt quite unwell in the evening. I got some fine Brandy

[page 67]
at Mr Plays, which did me good.
Sunday is a great day here—it seemed to be the best trad-ing day with the storekeepers. Go to church & buy

goods—Mex. fashion Fisher mentioned having sold "so many saints" as if they were Kegs of Nails. [80]

Nov 10th Monday. My man Young, not giving me satisfaction, & wishing to return, I let him go, & paid him off today. The scenery along Moro valley is quite beautiful— handsome meadows, covered with stock & high mountains gently sloping downwards.

Nov 11th Tuesday. I expected to start to Santa Fé this morning with Mr W Bransford who went over to Fort Union, & as he did not return, I defer my starting. The weather today & for two days past has been truly delightful, warm & balmy & bracing. Mountain air is charming & invigorating. It is very similar to the air in Virginia Mounts which I visited this summer.

[page 68]

Mr B arrived & reports that an express had reached Fort Union asking for troops to be sent over to Bent's Fort, as there had been fighting with the Indians (Kioways) & one of them had been shot, & danger of the people being murdered. So I can thank my stars I am out of it. [81]

Nov 12th Wednesday After making hasty preparations we left Moro for Santa Fe. Mr Wm A. Bransford having four little girls under his charge going to the convent in Santa Fé—[82] they may be called halfbreeds being the most of them children of Mexican women. I took two of them in my carriage, & was much bothered before we reached our destination. We had a Mexican who rode my horse, & we shared in the expense of paying him, as he worked for us both. Mr. Jos Play was very kind & polite to me—I remained in his house eating & sleeping there for several days, & he would not

[page 69]

accept one cent pay—he also freighted my goods over to
Santa Fe, for which he charged me nothing—a rare speci-
men I may say here—as almost every one seems to do fa-
vors—in hopes of getting pay. The Rio Moro is about 70
miles long & increases in width to its junction with the
Cañadiano After making 27 miles, we reached "Las
Vegas"[83] & went to the house of the Padre or Priest,
where we remained for the night. He entertained us very
hospitably, brot out his wines & seemed to be quite a bon
vivant. He was formerly a French soldier, & changed from
that to a Priest—but is certainly more fit for the former.[84]
I drank some Mexican wine with him—& was quite sick
afterwards—with pain & frequent discharges. After taking
some paregoric[85] I was relieved. Nov 13th [written later
over 14th] Travelled 12 miles

[page 70]

to Tecalote[86] & paid Moore & Rees[87] a visit—they are
pushing, active men & probably making much money.
From there we went to San Miguel & stopped for the
night at a Mexican hotel, rather a poor apology.[88]
Nov 14th [written later over 15th] Friday Travelled to near
Pecos an ancient village of Peublos, where are the remains
of an old cathedral—supposed to be some 400 years old.
The village is famed for the residence of a singular race of
Indians, of whom many curious legends are told. In their
temple they were said to keep an immense serpent to which
they sacrificed human beings [previous word crossed out in
ms.] victims. others say they worshipped a perpetual fire
that they believed to have been kindled by Montezuma, &
that one of their race was yearly appointed to watch the

fire. As the severity of the vigil always caused the death of
the watcher, in time this tribe became extinct.

[page 71]

It is said Montezuma promised to return to them in 400
years, if the fire was kept up—but as it is now out—it's
probable he will not keep his word.[89] The church has
been quite an imposing edifice, & even now in its ruins
looms up & seems to indicate that the builders were supe-
rior to the present stupid race of Mexicans. It is built in
the form of a cross, & indicates some taste in the builders.
We stopped at Jim Greys house,[90] a very comfortable
place, where we enjoyed very good fare.
Nov 15th [written later over 16th] Saturday. After travelling 4 or 5 miles we reached a cañon with hills on each
side from 1000 to 2000 feet above the road which continues to a point about 14 miles from Santa Fé.[91] The
road in some places was awful, running over rocks & thro'
a creek winding along the ravine. About 4 oclock we entered Santa Fé,[92] & after leaving our girls at the convent

[page 72]

went to the Fonda or Exchange—a one story adobe Hotel
situated on a corner opposite the Plaza or public square in
the center of the city.[93] The house is very well kept—
their table being really excellent, supplied with almost
every thing the country affords—immense onions, beets,
cabbages, rather small potatoes &c. The fare is high being
$2.50 per day for board & lodging & $1.00 per horse—
rather costly. After brushing up, I met [previous word
crossed out in ms.] went to Dr Connelly's store,[94] having a
letter to him, & met Mr Amberg his partner, a very polite

German gent, with whom I supped. After tea Mr Brittingham, a clerk of Dr C's[95] introduced me to a number of citizens & officers congregated at the Fonda, which is the
place of rendevous for the better class of Americans.
There is a large barroom attached to the house, & also
one large gambling room, & one or two private ones. In
one there was a game of Monte & a goodly number of
players. The Mexicans

[page 73]
have a great passion for gambling, & will sometimes play
off their last coat or blanket, so excited do they become.
The inscriptions at each end of the large gaming room are
[remainder of this passage unfinished in ms., but one and
one-half lines are left vacant in an otherwise closely written diary]
I accompanied a number of gents to a Fandango or party.
The women laid aside their "rebosas" or large mantillas
that they wear over their heads, & dress much like our females. While sitting they wear their fine shawls, partly
thrown over their heads, & quietly smoke their cigaritos.
Waltzing forms the chief part of their dansing. The principal one tonight was the Cumbé. After the dance the gents
take their partners out & treat them to a glass of wine or
candy. I retired early, being quite fatigued.
Nov 16th [written over 17th] Sunday. Santa Fé is elevated
about 6846 feet above the sea, situated

[page 74]
in a valley in the mountains—the latitude is near [pre-
vious word crossed out in ms.] 35 ° 44′06″, but as it is so
highly situated, the temperature is cooler than one would

expect. The houses are mostly built of adobes, one story high, & from a distance are hardly visible being the same color as the ground.

On the north side of the plaza or public square is what is termed the palace occupying the whole side of the square. On the remaining sides are stores of merchants & traders, & in the center is a tall flagstaff for the army flag. The country people congregate here to sell their marketing, corn &c, brot in on their "burros" or jackasses—the loads being tied on each side. They sometimes look quite ludicrous—a Mexican being seated back just near the tail.

[page 75]

Stores are kept open here on Sundays & a lively business done. After church I saw a great many of the Mex. women, who seem to think it all important to attend church, no matter what they do before or after. The morals of the residents generally are very bad—the habits of the women very loose, & the men addicted to gaming & stealing.

In the afternoon I visited the state house a large stone building in process of erection—to be 3 stories high, & also the penitentiary, quite massive—both will be a credit to the country—as there is something American about them. We also stopped at Mr Millers[96] room, & found a number of young men playing cards.

Nov 17th Monday. Called at Mr Becks of Beck, Johnson & Co, & Webb & Kingsburys.[97] The waggons arrive & I leave my goods at Mr H Connelly's.

[page 76]

Mr Bransford returns today—he is a very clever man—bro't my freight over & did not charge me one cent.

18th & 19th Weather pleasant & delightful. Visited Maj
Albert Smith Paymaster U.S.A. & took dinner with him.
he entertained me very Kindly—I had a letter to him from
Jno R. Triplett.[98] He kindly invited me to join his mess
but I concluded to remain boarding at the hotel. Mr
Green[99] begins to board & lodge me for Sixty Dollars per
month, & no extras. Privileges of dining &c. my friends.
If absent 3 days or more no charge for board. [previous
sentence inserted later between preceding and following
lines] I dropped in at Col Graysons, who was witnessing a
cockfight—he is a perfect bonvivant & extremely fond of
fun. Has his food and lives very comfortably. Quite a
scene at his house among some of the officers &c. The
Col, Maj Reynolds & Lieut [blank in ms.], put on a lot of
skins & promenaded

[page 77]

over to the Fonda, where they had an Indian dance.
I took dinner with Mr Macrae.[100] In the evening went to
a surprise party at Judge Houghtons,[101] & found almost all
the American ladies & passed quite a pleasant evening.
Nov 20th Thursday. Quite a deep snow & one slay out.
Dined with Mr Amberg. Visited Fort Marcy—built during
the Mexican War on an eminence above the town—it is
now in ruins.[102] Saw quite a number of graves near there.
Deposited Two Hundred Dollars $200.00 with Connelly &
Amberg—to my credit.
Nov 21st Friday Attended a party at Lieut Wilkins, a very
delightful affair. Col Bonneville, Maj Thornton, Capt
Easton, Lieuts Clitz, O'Bannon & Howland, & Maj Nich-
ols were present; as also Gov Merriweather Squire Collins
&c. Quite a handsome supper was spread.[103]

[page 78]

Slept with Mr Mercer, (Maj Smith's clerk) & breakfasted with him on Saturday[104]

Nov. 22d Much snow on the ground six or eight inches deep.

Sunday Nov 23d Attended the Bishops church[105] in the morning. It is quite a large adobe building, but presents a poor appearance. There are a few seats ranged near one side, but the congregation generally kneel or stand. Called on Capt Easton, dined with Mr Amberg. In the evening Major Smith called for me to visit Mrs Wilkins & Mrs Macrae—[106] we did so & had quite a pleasant time. The Major is very kind & attentive to me, & I am very much pleased with him.

Monday 24th The mail arrived today quite unexpectedly, & caused quite an excitement.[107] I was very anxious to hear from home, went to the office & got nothing at all— & no news. Was much disappointed un-

[page 79]

til I saw Col St Vrain & Mr Alexander just in from Fort Union; they reported that my letters were sent by the Mail. I went back to the office & got a few papers, but no letters. Was much worried & after travelling around for some time finally discovered my letters in the barroom— Col St Vrain having brot them in himself. I rec'd long letters from my mother, father, brother & sister Maggy—& letters also from Boomer & Hynes. I was greatly gratified to get them, learning that all was well at home, & the other interesting news. My horse lost at Indian Creek, was never recovered. There had been a grand agricultural Fair in St. Louis—that attracted much attention.[108] Politics raging high in the States & prospects very certain of J Buchanans election as President.

[page 80]
I got also a dozen newspapers, & 3 periodicals, so that I can post myself up. Prospect of war again between Russia & Austria combined against England & France, on account of the latter wishing to force the King of Naples into certain measures—Russia advocating the Doctrine of the Divine Right of Kings. My cousin Jas Glasgow was soon to be married. I was to have been 1st groomsman— so I miss a new suit. There was a fandango at Lieut Clitzs but I did not attend.
Tuesday 25th Weather moderate—Rode out with Major Smith & felt quite unwell. Laid down & rested & in evening attended a party at Col Jno B. Graysons. There had been a debate previous to the party—the Literati Club,[109] & afterwards the Empire Club—whose members are

[page 81]
fined if they speak any sense. The party was pleasant. Was awakened by a party next door—late at night.
Wednesday Nov 26th—Nothing of note today. Plenty of snow. Wrote to G. B. Boomer.
Thursday Nov 27th Hearing of Maj Smith's intention of starting tomorrow for Albuquerque & Los Lunas, & having been invited to go along, I was much occupied in getting my letters written to my parents, to go per Mail of 1st Dec—so as to get off with him.
Friday Nov 28th I started for Albuquerque with Maj Smith, & his clerk, Mr Mercer, in a gov't ambulans, escorted by four soldiers—they are going to pay off troops.

Passed thro' Bernalillo, a very well built town, & stopped at Algedones for the night—42 Miles a very long drive thro' deep snow.

Saturday Nov 29th After striking the Del Norte River, which is quite a large stream

[page 82]

with a rapid current, we reached Albuquerque about 1 oclock, & I stopped with Dr DeLeon, Surgeon USA—a very clever gent. Met Capt Gibson, Col [previous word crossed out in ms.] Major Van Horn, M[a]j Ruskin & Lt Wright—clever gents.

Sunday Nov 30th Visited Maj Van Horn, & went to Church. Fandango at Chatto Armijos—Chatto & Huana.[110] Weather truly delightful here.

Monday Dec 1st Started back to Santa Fé the Maj concluding not to go to Los Lunas. Road bad, quite a snow, & weather cool. Stopped at Algedones.

Tuesday Dec 2d Arrived at Santa Fé, after a long & cold ride thro' deep snows—The trip down having proved a very pleasant one.

Wednesday Dec 3d Called on Dr Connelly. Attended a very pleasant party given by Mrs Dr Sloan U.S.A., & enjoyed it much. Previous to the party there was a fine Concert given by the 3d Infty Band—performance very good.[111] I escorted Mrs Lieut Wilkins to both.

Thursday Dec 4th The weather for days past has been excessively cold, but now pleasant.

[page 83]

I had no idea the winters were so severe here. In the evening Capt Easton & Mr Beck called & invited me to at-

tend a Baylé or Mexican Party at Col Graysons. I went &
found it a grand Fandango—Every one was there almost
(except the decent American ladies)—officers, gents,
gamblers & all with their mistresses. Champagne &c.
flowed in abundance & the party was a lively one. I was
soon satiated & tired of it—came away & retired.
Friday Dec 5th I sold my mules today to Mr Thos Bowler
(of the Exchange) for $250.00 & my harness for $15.00—
Say Total $265.00. It was advisable to let them go at that,
rather than hold, as their board was very high $12.00 per
Week. They had cost me say $325.00 adding board
$35.00—$360.00. So that the loss on them is near
$100.00, which I hope to make up on the sale of my am-
bulanse. Dined with Maj Smith—& went sleighriding
with him in the evening—he taking four Mexican ladies
along. Had a very pleasant time—Moonlight night. Visited Mrs Wilkins & MacRea this evening.

[page 84]
Dec 5th 1856
Finding the room I occupied too noisy from neighboring
gambling room, & proximity to Mr Tom Smith & Lady, I
moved to a room opening on the carrelle—a much more
pleasant one.
Saturday Dec 6/56 Weather continues very cold—went
sleighing in evening with Mrs Wilkins, Sloan & a large
party—very nice. Gambling tables are doing a grand business now at the Hotel—faro, Monté &c. A Lieut in the
army won $460.00 tonight.
Sunday Dec 7th Weather cold—visited Mrs Maj Nichols,
Mrs Sloan & Mrs Houghton. Went to a young mans room
& saw Drew & Smith in a pretty condition—[intoxicated]

Monday 8th Accompanied Bishop Lammi out to his
rancho about 3 miles—a very romantic & beautiful spot—
a large valley surrounded by mountains.
Tuesday 9th Rode with Dr Cavanaugh[112] in heavy snow.
Went sleighing in evening with Mrs Sykes & co., & attended the meeting

[page 85]
of the Debating Society of Santa Fe. Afterwards had a
danse at Mrs Wilkins.
Wednesday 10th. Heard Lieut O'Bannon tell of about 130
Recruits of whom 60 loaded their muskets ball first—a fire
occurred in their camp on the plains & as only part of the
guns went off it was discovered the "green uns" did not
understand their calling.[113] He also spoke of his Regiment
having bought out a Major [blank in ms.] for $2300.00, to
get him out of the army—he being very disagreeable.
Thursday Dec 11th. The Court Martial for trial of Capt
McLean met yesterday—a large number of officers in attendance.[114] Attended a very pleasant party at Lieut
O'Bannons in the evening.
Friday Dec 12th. Weather today warm & balmy. It has
been very cold here for some time. Felt rather unwell today, but after my evening ride, was much better.
I took my horse from the Fonda stable yesterday,

[page 86]
Dec 12th 1856
& keep him in company with Dr Kavanaugh we sharing
the expense.
Saturday 13th Dec Weather very cold again. Attended the

Court Martial today—it consisted of a body of fine looking officers. Peeped thro' a gents curtain in afternoon—queer sight. Thermometer down to 15 ° above 0.
Sunday 14th. Ther. 10 ° above zero. The news came today by Southern express of Buchanan's election as President of the U.S. over Fillmore & Fremont.
Monday 15th. Attended a delightful party given by Col Bonneville—it was a very handsome affair far surpassing what I expected to see here. The ladies were dressed beautifully, & the officers in full dress—epaulets & sashes presented a fine appearance. Previous to the party I supped with the Padre, & had a pleasant time. Tuesday 16th. Weather moderated & pleasant. Attended the meeting of the Litterary society at Col Graysons, & afterwards went to a Fandango—a pretty good ballé—left early & retired.

[page 87]

Dec 17 1856
Wednesday Dec 17th Attended the Concert in the evening. Thursday 18th Went to a fine party given by Judge Houghton—the supper was elegant, & would have done justice to a city affair. Friday 19th & 20th Nothing of much interest.
Sunday 21st I indulged my appetite by eating a piece of mince pie at the hotel, & taking a violent ride afterwards felt unwell. My room smoked very much at night—but I did not discover where the smoke came from, until Mr Green came in & found out that one of the beams near the chimney was on fire. After throwing water on it, knocking the mud thro' &c, it was put out. I might have suffocated, had I gone to bed & the smoke increased.
Monday 22d Rather unwell. Rode in evening & felt much

better after it. Weather delightful.
Tuesday 23d Took pills but they did not operate well.
Went to a pleasant party at Maj Smiths.
Wednesday 24th Delightful day. The mail arrived today
about 2 oclock from States

[page 88]
Dec 24th/ 56
bringing me a number of letters reporting all well at home.
I got my letters about dark, & as I was disappointed at first
in not finding any (the Fort Union mail not being opened
untill late), I appreciated them highly equal to so many
Christmas Presents, which are scarce for me here. Christ-
mas Day Thursday
Dec 25th. Went visiting the ladies quite pleasant time.
Had Maj Smith to dine with me. Made presents of money
to some of the Hotel Servants, & may say I got off
cheap—compared to what it would be in the States. Fri-
day 26th Dec Snowy & blustery day. Dined with Mr.
Robb.
Sat 27th at Maj Smiths—rather unwell.
Sunday 28th Dec. Charming weather. I consulted Dr.
Sloan about going to San Antonio Texas, & from there to
Virginia—He seemed to think it would benefit me about
as much as staying here.

[page 89]
Dec 28th 56
I now think of going down in the 1st Feby Mail to San
Antonio. Busy writing home.
Dec 29th rather unwell today.

Dec 30th Tuesday. I was called in today by Maj Albert
Smith, Pay Master of the U.S. Army, who offered me the
situation of clerk with him. The pay being good, & work
light & not very confining, I accepted it—and am soon to
enter on my new duties.
My having taken the new offer, of course caused me to
change my plans, concerning my southern trip, & I now
expect to return with him in the spring to the States.
Quite a snow storm today.
The last mail brot intelligence of the Election of
Buchanan & Breckinridge for President & Vice P. of
U.S., and this evening some of the Democracy turned
out, & had a grand torch light procession, & glorification
meeting. The plaza was

[page 90]

Dec 30/56
lit up with a large number of fires the Palace of the Governors illuminated & cannon roaring in the Square, with
the fine music of the 3d Infty Band in all quite a grand affair for S. Fe.
Dec 31st Wednesday. Maj Smith having business at Fort
Union, starts over there today & I with him to pay off the
troops. We have an escort of ten men, & travel in with
[previous word crossed out in ms.] a Gov. ambulanse with
four mules. Mr. G Alexander in company. Ground covered with snow. Arrived at Grey's or "Roseville" about 5
oclock P.M., & remained over night. This is the last day
of my partnership in business with my father—the time
(two years) having now expired.
Here I am away out in the wilderness, away from so many
of the comforts &c. of city life at the close of this eventful

year. How things change! One year ago, I little expected
to find myself here. 1856 has expired

[page 91]
[From this point on, the diary is written in black or brown
ink with a fine steel pen.]
January 1857
Jan 1st Thursday. This day which at home is devoted to
social visiting, I passed travelling from Grey's to Las
Vegas, a distance of near 50 miles. We paid one call at
Tecoloté, but it was not very fashionable. Stopped at Mr
Boyce's[115] at Vegas, & were well cared for—a capital
place. I heard there was to be a fancy ball in the
evening—a select affair, I went & found it miserably com-
mon & dirty—Men dansing in their shirt sleeves &c,
Came home quite satisfied with it.
Today my engagement with Major Albert J. Smith, Pay
Master of the U.S. Army, as his clerk, commences, salary
to be [blank in ms.].
Jan 2d Started about 8 1/2 oclock from Vegas & reached
Fort Union[116] about 2 oclock; I went to Mr. G. Alex-
ander's store & am to stay with him the Maj. being at
Capt Jones'. Fort Union is beautifully situated on a large
plain, protected on both sides by mts. It is a U.S. Military
Post

[page 92]
Jan 1857
but is not built as a regular Fort. The houses, dwellings for
officers & soldiers, are built of logs (filled up with mud), &
present quite a handsome appearance, with their white-
washed fronts, compared to the mud houses of the "Me-

tropolis" Santa Fe. I met Col. Loring, Capts Hatch, McLain, Morris & Jones, & Shoemaker, Lt. Ransome, Jones, Tracy & Capt McFerran[.] In the evening I called on Miss Freddy Jones.

Jan 3d Saturday. In the morning I commenced my work with Major Smith at Dr. Leathermans House, making out pay accounts & pay rolls; It is a rather tedious & confining operation. I am invited to Capt. Llewellyn Jones' to dinner, which I attend. He gave a handsome entertainment—the Blanc Mange,[117] Pure cream & delicious sweet-meats, reminding me of city life. His daughter Miss Fred as she is called is a very lovely lady, & gave us some capital songs. I passed the time very agreeably. In the evening there was a raffle at the Sutlers store, for a horse of

[page 93]

Jan 1857

Capt McLains, which he had won himself. Quite a jolly time among those interested.

Jany 4th Sunday. The mail arrived yesterday for the States—Mr Beck a passenger—It went off early this morning—on its risky journey.[118] I am much occupied making out the pay rolls, & do not have much leisure today. Almost missed my dinner. I sup with Lt. Ransome. Monday Jan.

5th Being ready with our Roll, we commenced paying off the troops, we paid Capt Jones Compy., Capt Hatch & the Band—the pay'ts. amounting to near $10,000.00. After we got thro' I dined with Lt. Ransome, & started almost immediately off for Las Vegas, which we reached about 6 o'clock P.M., & stopped at Dr. Boyce's where we were kindly entertained.

Jan 6th Tuesday. Travelled from Vegas, via Tecolote, &
San Miguel (having got on the wrong road) to Jim
Grey's (Roseville), where we arrived about dark, & passed
quite a pleasant evening, the hostess being quite agreeable. Found nothing to eat in San M. but little pumkin
pies poor—

[page 94]

Jan 1857
Jan 7th Wednesday. Started early from Grey's, and trudged
our way up to the Mts.—it snowing very hard. We got out
of the ambulans, going up one terribly bad mountain, &
walked up. I was very much fatigued, & after getting back
into the carriage suffered considerably from cold. We arrived in Santa Fe about one o'clock & dined at the Fonda.
I attended the weekly concert of the Band in the evening.
Jan 8th Thursday. I had my baggage &c., moved over
from the Fonda this morning to Major Smith's office,
where I intend sleeping. At work on Pay Rolls Capt
Elliot's Co, &c. Col Greyson had a celebration celebrating
the day—Battle N. Orleans. Snowed almost incessantly
today.
Jan 9th. Changed desk & Beds in the office where I
sleep—weather very cold.
Jan 10th Saturday. Snow about 8 inches deep, but weather
now clear & pleasant. Bo't pair of blue mil[itary] pants.
Paid Dr. Kavanagh $16.62 being for food &c. for my

[page 95]

Jan 10th 1857
horse kept in his stable to date—for one month, being
much cheaper than keeping him at the Fonda.

Received Fifty Dollars ($50.00) of Green & Bowler on a/c
of mules sold them
Jan 11th Sunday. Weather clear & very cold. Mail from
Taos reports snow there 4 ft Deep. Visited Mrs Wilkins in
evening. Lt. OBannon having meat stolen out of the
placita, put arsenic in a piece of mutton, & it was stolen
last night. Unlucky thief who eats it.
Jan 12th Monday. Engaged today working on Abstract of
Payments to be sent to Washn. [Washington]
Jan 13th Tuesday Weather warm & pleasant. There passed
before our house today the funeral of a child perhaps three
years old. The dead body was exposed on an open bier carried by four women—some of them laughing & talking—
it was dressed in its usual clothing—& its face was plainly
visible. A small boy preceded the bier carrying

[page 96]
Jan 13th 1857
a cross, and behind followed a man playing gay & lively
tunes on a violin. The whole procession numbered six or
seven people. These poor Mexicans seem rather like half
civilized, than otherwise.[119]
After seeing the funeral, we took a ride, & were joined by
the Padre, who likely had said the ceremony over the
child. He was in gay spirits & full of fun. His pony almost
lost in the deep Snow.
Jan 14th. Weather delightful
Jan 15th. Supped with Amberg, & rode out twice today—
weather lovely as spring. Paid Monicho[?] $1.75 for at-
tending to my pony. Was asked into Mrs Wilkins to get
some cake & frozen custard. Bowels slightly loose having
taken two pills (14th).

Jan 16th Quiet & dull.
Jany 17th Weather cold again. I at-

[page 97]
tended a Ballé given at the Fonda this evening—quite re-
cherché.
Jan 18th Sunday. Read the Letter written to me by my
mother & by her put in the Bible she presented to me. It
is a valuable letter, containing excellent advice such as a
mother can give. Called on Mrs. Wilkins & Mrs Dr Sloan
& presented them with some dd [dried] ginger.
Jan 19th Monday (January 14th Received of Bowler &
Green $100.25 being balance due me per their bill, & ac-
count, closing board bill & sale of mules.)
Jan 19th Monday I have made arrangements with Mr J.H.
Dunn to teach me Spanish. He to give me five lessons a
week.[120] I paid him in advance yesterday five Dollars for
fifteen lessons. He commences teaching me tonight.
Jan 21st Wednesday. We today had a din-

[page 98]
Jan 21st 1857
ner party at our house, attended by Judge Brocchus, U.S.
Supreme Judge, Col J.B. Grayson & Major Whilden. The
time passed off very pleasantly. Major Whilden went rid-
ing to the Fonda. Concert in the evening.
Jan 22d Thursday. Weather delightful. Not very well today.
Jan 24th Saturday Invited Major Nichols, Capt Gibson, &
Mr MCRae to dine with us today, which they accordingly
did. I attended a fandango in the evening, but only staid a
short time.

Jan 25th Sunday. Charming day. The Southern Mail arrived today, but the Eastern Mail has not yet arrived, altho' anxiously looked for.[121] Col. B.L.E. Bonneville took tea with us.

Jan 26th Monday. I drew my money out of Connelly & Amberg's hands today.

[page 99]
Jan 26/56 [Larkin writes the wrong year]
The amount (including money for goods sold them) was Two Hundred & Thirty one Dollars ($231.00) thereby balancing our a/cs to this date. I have today deposited with Messrs. Beck, Johnson & Co, merchants of Santa Fe—Two Hundred & Forty Dollars $240.00, which amount is to my credit & subject to my order.

Jan 27th Tuesday I sold my ambulanse today to Thos F Bowler of Santa Fé for $280.00, being about $80.00 over what it cost in St. L. I thereby lose but little by my sale of mules, as the loss on them is in a measure balanced by gain on mules. [i.e., the gain on the carriage]

The Total Sale to Bowler am.— $545.00
"   do   Cost Mules & Ambul. $547.00
I attended the meeting of the Literary Club tonight, & heard some excellent essays.

[page 100]
Jan 28th 1857
Wednesday 28th. Thos F Bowler paid me today for my Ambulanse say $280.00, which amount I deposited to my credit with Beck, Johnson & Co, making Total Amo. to my credit there $520.00 (Five Hundred & Twenty Dol-

lars) Jan 29th Thursday Mail not yet arrived. I attended
the meeting of the Senate of N.M. which closed this evening. It is not a very brilliant body.
Pay [Perea?] $1.00 for washing clothes
Jan 30th Friday I make out Wm Bent's Account, showing
my balance due him $188.75, & send same to my father
to get it attended to. I invited Dr Boyce of Las Vegas & Dr
Kavanaugh to dine with me today. Met Mr Idler this evening, agent of the Placer Mining Company. [122]

[page 101]
Jan 31st 1857 Saturday. Wrote to my father & John S Pim
requesting latter to purchase 1200 @ $1500.00 worth of
land at $1.25 @ 5.00 per acre in Minnesota or Wiscon-
sin[.] Drew my pay as Pay Master's Clerk viz

Pay per Month	$58.33
Subsistence 31 rations @ 75c.	23.25
Making Total	$81.58

to this date for Month of January.
I deposited with Beck & Johnson today Eighty Dollars
($80.00), making to my credit on their books $600.00. I
learned this morning thro' Mr. Hibran formerly clerk at J
& W.R. Bernards Westport that my lost horse returned to
Westport or neighborhood, and have written Messrs. B. &
H Clay Tate to take measures to secure him, & send him
to St. Louis, & to draw on THL & Co. [Thomas H.
Larkin & Co.] for charges on him.

[page 102]
[At the end of the 1856–57 diary is a single page of notes
and a page of accounts.]

119

Memos—*outward bound*
Oct 13th. I left in charge and care of Mr Wm W Bent
(Bent's Fort) for safe keeping Two Hundred and Thirty
Dollars in Gold $230.00
Sep 25th I gave J & W. R. Bernard of Westport Mo a Dft
on T. H. Larkin & Co for $435.00 Four Hundred Thirty
Five Dollars—being for Mules, Horses & sundries bo't of
them. I also left Dft favor Riddlesbarger & Co for $23.00
Twenty Three Dollars, being for Freight on goods & car-
riage per "Morning Star" to Kansas, & they were to col-
lect their commission as charges on my trunk & valise
sent back to St Louis.
N Dec 5/56 [Larkin started to write November] Sold my 2
Mules for $250.00 & Harness for $15.00 to Thos. Bowler
Santa Fe.
Jan 28/57 Sold my Ambulase to Thos Bowler Santa Fe for
$280.00 Cash.

[pages 103 and 104 blank in ms.]

[page 105]
a/c of Jas Young—
Employed Jas Young—as driver &c. at $25.00 per
Month—from Sep 25–56
Paid him	Date		Amount
	October	1st	$10.00
	do	25th	$15.00
	Nov 8		$11.62

[Note: pages 106 and 107 are diary entries made during
the week before Larkin contracted his fatal pneumonia
(January 1875), and are here included.]

[page 106]

January 1875

1. snow. dreary morning. Took Annie to Dr. Hereford's office, he burned the dog bite with *luna costic* [lunar caustic] Powders—A. had fever all day—
2. Mr. L. to city.
3. Beautiful day Mary (cook), Maggie and myself to high mass—M. remained at school. Fathers Early and Coppins called.
4. Right cold—Ther 10 below Freezing. Mr. L. and myself to city on second train. Snow—Jessie & myself at home on 4 o'clk. train—Mr. l. remained in[?]
5. Terribly cold. Jessie to the convent. called on Widow Smith. Letter from Tommie, wrote to him.
6. Still very cold—Mr.L. home. In town since Monday.

[page 107]
7. Mr. L. to city—not so cold—tries to snow.

Appendix 1:
Inventory of Goods

The following list is a copy of Larkin's inventory of goods and equipment carried with him on the trail to Santa Fe in 1856, diary pages four through eight. Also included is a list of the persons to whom he carried letters of introduction, and a transcription of the letter of introduction Larkin had his cousins, Glasgow & Brother, prepare for Santa Fe traders Webb & Kingsbury.

[page 4]
List of Articles purchased for the trip—& prices

1 Buffalo Robe	7 00
1 Indian Rubber cape	5 "
2 Pair Sup [erior?] Blue Blankets $11.00 pc.	22 "
3 Pair W. P. [water proof] Boots 2/7.50	17 50
1—10.00	
1 " Shoes	3 50
2 " Sheets, 1 Pillow	
2 Pillow cases	
1 Military Over Coat	17 "
2 Pair Thick Pantaloons	
1 " Black do	

2 New Heavy Coats
4 Heavy Red flan Shirts
3 Calico Shirts
3 Hickory do
4 Pairs Red Flan Drawers
6 " Socks
Saddle Blanket   1.50
1 Pistol Belt
1 Gal   Black Lead for carriage [?]

[page 5]

1 Finlays Ambulans	$202.00
1 Pair Harness & Straps &c.	26.00
2 Mules	325.00
1 Horse	100.00
1 Saddle	25.00
1 Bridle with 2 Bits	7 "
1 Pair Holsters	7.50
2 Long Straps 6 ft	.75
1 Pair Spurs	1.50
2 Worn Bed Covers	
1 Knife Scabbard	.30
1 Gun Strap	
3 Picket Ropes 30 ft ea	
1 Pistol Colts Army Revolver	29 "
1 " Small Pocket	17.50
1 Hawkins Rifle	28 "
1 Double Bbl Shot Gun	
1 Bullet Pouch	2.25
1 Shot do	2.25
1 Bullet Ladle	
3 " Moulds	
1 Tar Can & Strap	.75

[page 6]

1 Whet Stone		.20
2 Hatchets	75 ea	1.50

1 Case Laflins   Dia. Gun Powder   12.00
1 Bdl [bundle?] Bar Lead   25#   7c [cents]   1.75
1 Cedar Bucket   1 "
1 5 Gal Iron Bound Keg
1 Glass Lanthorn $2.50   1 "
¼ Box Star Candles   2.40
1 [do.] Elys Per Caps W.P. [waterproof]   Sm   1.40
3   "   "   "   "   "   Large   2.25   6.75
4 Boxes Gun Wads   1 "
5 Boxes Buck Shot Cartri[d]ges
4 Extra Nipples   S G [shot gun?]   1.75
10 Pds No 5 Shot   }
 5   "   " 6 do }_____   2.00
10   "   " Goose do   }
2 Boxes Wax Matches   .60
1 Camp Kettle 2 gals }
1 Small Skillet   }
1 Tin Coffee Pot   }_____   3.35
4 Tin Cups   }
6 Tin Plates over [sic] }

                              [page 7]
1 Stew Pan with cover   ½ Gal   }
1 Frying Pan   }
1 Pepper Box   back [sic]   }
½ Doz Knives & Forks   2.25
1 Iron Cook Spoon   .25
2 Table Spoons   10   .20
2 Bags Flour   100# ea
3 Sides Bacon   [crossed out]
6 Hams   [crossed out]
40 Pds Coffee
40   " Crushed Sugar
1 Bag [Daisy/Dairy?] Salt
1 # Gro[und] Pepper
1 Coffee Mill
1 Box Pilot Bread
1   "   Butter Crackers

½ Doz   Yeast Powder
1 Powder Horn
1   ″   Flask
1 Canteen & Strap   .75
1 Keg I[?] H[?] Syrup

[page 8]
1 Sup[erior?] Opera Glass   16.00
1 In[dia] Rubber Blanket   3.50
4 Merino Shirts   @1.50   6 ″
2 Wool Comforts   50 c[ents]   1 ″
1 Bottle Pain Killer   .50
Hawling goods from Kan[sas] to Wes[t]port   3 ″
Repairing overcoat   1.75
Flannel for do   1 ″
8 Bus Green Apples   75   6 ″
3 ″ Potatoes   @1   3 ″
Hawling goods   1.50
1 Kit White Fish   5 ″
10 Doz Eggs   15   1.50
Sacks, Boxes & Trunks   8 ″
1 Thermometer   1 ″
1 Plush Case   2.50
3 Pairs Inside Soles   .90
8 Bushels Corn   10.00
1 Indian Pony at Bent's Fort   75.00
[later addition in black ink]
WW Bent frt on 1100# to Moro   154.00

[page 9]
Have Letters of Introduction[1] to Mess.
Riddlesbarger & Co Kansas, & J & W.R. Ber-
nard—Westport—& also to
Major Albert Smith paymaster U.S.A.   N. Mex.
Dr. A. T. Ridgely   U.S.A.   Fort Riley   New Mex.
Hon[orable] Dr Henry Connelly   Santa Fe
Webb & Kingsbury   do

Jas L. Collins	do
Macmanus & Miller	Chihuahua N. M.
Mr. Beck (of Beck Johnson & Co)	Santa Fe
Hon Judge Houghton	"
Mr Mercure of J. & H. Mercure	"
Rev'd Wm Smith (Baptist Miss)	
Dr Steck (Indian Agent)	N. Mexico
Hugh Stephenson	El Paso Texas
Judge Beaubien	Fernando de Taos N. Mex.
Col C St Vrain	Fort Union New Mexico

Letter of Introduction [2]

St. Louis September 17, 1856

Messrs. Webb & Kingsbury
Santa Fe
Gent[lemen]

We take pleasure in introducing to your favorable acquaintance our friend and relative Mr. James Ross Larkin of this city who visits New Mexico for the purpose of improving his health. Any attention you may show Mr. L. will be gratefully appreciated & reciprocated by us. Should Mr. L. require any money his drafts upon his house here will be promptly paid.
Very respectfully yours,
Glasgow & Brother

Notes

1. Of the numerous persons to whom Larkin carried letters, he did not contact the following men, or else did not record any meeting with them: Riddlesbarger & Co., a Kansas mercantile firm; Dr. A. T. Ridgely, Fort Riley; Macmanus & Miller, Chihuahua merchants; Reverend William Smith, Baptist Missionary; Dr Michael Steck, Indian Agent; Hugh Stephenson, of El Paso; and Judge Carlos Beaubien, of Fernando de Taos. Among these men, Steck, Beaubien and Stephenson are the most prominent. Michael Steck became Indian agent and later superintendent of Indian affairs under governor David Meriwether (Meriwether,

My Life in the Mountains and on the Plains, 159 n.). Hugh Stephenson was a merchant at El Paso, and may have lived there since about 1829 (Barry, *Beginning of the West,* 148, 1229). Carlos Beaubien was a Canadian who came to New Mexico in 1823, married the daughter of a prominent New Mexican family, Paula Lobato, and lived at Taos. Beaubien became Lucien B. Maxwell's father-in-law (Twitchell, *The Leading Facts of New Mexican History,* 2: 273). Of those he did contact, J & W. R. Bernard of Westport have been treated in a note to the diary, as have Dr. Henry Connelly, James L. Collins, Preston Beck, Jr., and Judge Joab Houghton, all of Santa Fe. Ceran St. Vrain also appears in a note to the diary, above. The Mercure brothers, Joseph and Henri, were traders at Santa Fe. Webb & Kingsbury was the largest firm in the region, and Larkin kept an account with them during his visit to Santa Fe. Major Albert Smith was the U.S. army paymaster for whom Larkin worked.

2. Copy of letter in Missouri Historical Society, folder 9–17–1856, Webb Collection, M.H.S.

Appendix 2:
Newspaper Accounts

The following are three newspaper articles taken from the *Santa Fe Weekly Gazette* from 1856–57 that either were written from materials provided to the newspaper by Larkin, or mention his activities, or refer to the incidents that occurred at Bent's Fort after Larkin left for Santa Fe.

"News From Bent's Fort"

November 26, 1856

From Mr. Larkin who arrived in town a few days since, from Bent's Fort, on the Arkansas, we learn that a difficulty had occurred with Mr. Bent, the proprietor of the Fort, and a party of Kiowa Indians, which was likely to terminate very seriously. It seems that Bent after his return from the States, found it necessary to discharge one of his men. As this man was a friend of the Kiowas they took his part, and one of the chiefs used insulting language to Bent in reference to his discharge, for which he was chastised, this aroused the whole party, and but for the Cheyennes, who came to the assistance of Bent, he would in all probability have been killed, and his property destroyed. In the difficulty which occurred between the parties, one of the Kiowas was shot, this served to exasperate them still further, until the quarrel became so serious as to induce Mr. Bent to despatch the greater portion of his goods to the town of Mora, in Taos county, for security. He also sent to Fort Union for soldiers to protect him in making his retreat from the Indian country. Mr. Larkin left the Fort with the wagons that brought in Bent's goods. From Mr. Joseph Doyle, we learn, that after the departure of Mr. Larkin, the Cheyennes made an attack on a party of Kiowas and took from them some forty head of horses, and drove the Indians off to the south. From the last accounts the Cheyennes had started in pursuit of another party of Kiowas with the avowed intention of "wiping them out."

Mr. Doyle who is well acquainted with the Indians of the plains, thinks it will be very unsafe for small parties of traders to attempt to cross the plains in the spring; this we understand is also the opinion of Mr. Bent, than whom perhaps no one has more knowledge of the Indians. It is certainly time the government had taken some steps to protect our traders against these Indians; they seem to have lost all respect for our people, and unless they are chastised and made to fear the power of the government, we had as well surrender the peaceable occupation of the plains to them, and give up all communication with our friends in the States.

"Military Affairs"

January 17, 1857

The command under Lt. McRae, Rifles, returned to Fort Union from Bent's Fort, on the 8th inst[ant]. It is understood the following information was obtained there in relation to the Kiowas, Cheyennes and Arapahoes. On the 9th of September last, "Sitting Bear," a Kiowa chief, with fifty, or sixty men, armed—went to the Fort and forced the man in charge to give him two barrels of sugar, and seven, or eight barrels of hard bread, of the subsistence stores there deposited. He also took some cloth from the store—on the 26th October ten or twelve of the principal men (Kiowas) went to the Fort to have a "talk" with Mr. Bent—he told them to leave—"Eagle Tail," one of their chiefs, following him menacingly from room to room, Mr. Bent fired at him. The Kiowas then ran off—were pursued by the Cheyennes, and some of their horses taken. On the first November forty or fifty Kiowas came up, and commenced firing towards the Fort. The Cheyennes drove them off, wounding two.—On the 19th December "Sitting Bear," with a small party went to the Cheyenne village, near the Fort and tried to prevail upon the Cheyennes not to be at peace with the whites. This chief is the principal one of the Kiowas, and has great influence with the young men—"Little Mountain," another chief of influence among the Kiowas, and who has 30 or 40 lodges in his band, is well disposed towards the whites, and says that "Sitting Bear" cannot be controled [sic]—and in case of a fight with the whites he himself would have nothing to do with it. The Kiowas number 250 or 300 lodges—5 or 600 men, and from 1000 to 1500 women and children—they are considered the best armed and mounted of all the Indians of the plains. They nearly all have firearms— mostly the smooth bored German fusil, of which they were furnished with seventy or eighty last summer at the payment of their annuity. They are also well supplied with revolvers and dragoon pistols—they are all mounted. These Indians extend their forays far down into Texas, and into Chihuahua, and are often found in company with the Comanches. They are now on the Cimmarron [sic] river—their villages scattered along the valley from the Independence road to Crooked Creek. . . . The Cheyennes on the Arkansas number about 300 lodges . . . although at peace now with the Kiowas, they have no good feeling towards them— there is no reason for this dislike, except that, regarding Bent's Fort as a place of trade for themselves and the Arapahoes, they do not wish it interfered with, and they rather consider the Kiowas as intruders on their hunting grounds. The Arapahoes are about

Appendix 2

equal in number to the Cheyennes—and their relations with the Kiowas are similar to those of the Cheyennes.

"Arrivals From the States"

July 11, 1857

From Mr. J. K. [sic] Larkin, who returned a short time since from the States, we learn that the following gentlemen, with their families, have within a few days past, arrived at Fort Union. Mr. Geo. Alexander and lady, Mr. Samuel Humphreys and lady, of Kentucky, Mr. Geo. Collier and lady, of St. Louis, and Doctor T. L. Bancroft of New Madrid, Mo.

These gentlemen, we understand, with the exception of Mr. Alexander, who resides at Fort Union, crossed the plains on a trip of pleasure, and in pursuit of health. Doctor Connelly and Col. St. Vrain, citizens of the Territory, with Mr. H. F. Brittingham, and Mr. Geo. Smith, also returned.

The following trains got in during the present week: Messrs. Spiegelberg & Co., 26 wagons, Messrs. Connelly and Amberg, 10 wagons, Messrs. Webb & Kingsbury, 23 wagons, Messrs. Beck and Johnson, 26 wagons. Other trains are close at hand and will be here in a few days.

Appendix 3:
Letters From James Ross Larkin to
M. M. Broadwell of Kansas City, Missouri,
April and May 1866

St. Louis Apl 11/66

Dear Broadwell—

I am nearly sick & used up, & had it not been for wishing to attend to your Douglas matter I believe I would have shut myself up at home, but anxious to get it closed & the Notes discounted as promised me I kept up.

I saw Pollard [?] & Renick [?] again & they wouldn't vouch that paper even with the R & G [?] name added. After learning that I tho't it a good operation at 1 & 1 1/4.

Douglas spoke of leaving [illegible] I forward Receipts & Insurance Policies to cover amo[unt] cash Pay[ment?] but concluded to let that stand until 17 Inst[ant] when he will pay up & get his deed. He says there is a small judgement against Jacob P. Broadwell to be removed which he says you will attend to. It is something connected with the Allen matter. If it were not for the Cholera coming I would be greatly tempted to take that Plains Trip with you, & it won't be difficult to persuade me even now, as I am greatly under the weather. Will write if anything important occurs but expect you soon back. Yours Very Truly,

Jas. R. Larkin

I got the [illegible] your papers in our safe.

St. Louis Apl 16/66

Mr. M. M. Broadwell
Kansas City, Mo.
Dear Sir
    Your valued favor of 12 Inst[ant] rec'd. & today we remit to Mr.
A. H. Pomroy & Co New York Dft[draft] on N.Y. for

$$\begin{array}{r} \$11,000.00 \\ \$1.75 \text{ per M[thousand] Ex.} \\ \underline{\$19.25} \end{array}$$

To Your Debit: $11,019.25
[letter damaged] will pay [letter damaged]

Yours Very Truly,
Thos. H. Larkin & Co.

N.B. I am feeling better, & have now consent to go on a trip, but
to what point am not decided, either Plains or Europe. Hope soon
to hear from you, & to hear of your improved health.

James R. Larkin

St. Louis Apl 18/66

M. M. Broadwell Esq.
Kansas City, Mo.
Dear Sir
    We yesterday received of Jno [John] I. [?] Douglas Esq amo[unt]
Cash Pay't due 2^d Inst[allment] * $15,274.69
        & 15 days Interest @ 8 %   50.88
Making to yr cr. & subject to order   Total $15,325.57
& gave him the Deed from J. P. Broadwell & his old Notes &
a/ct.
Douglas memo indicates $4.00 more than yours, & he thinks it
correct & paid accordingly. He signed the Receipt you wrote.

Yours Very Truly,
Thos. H. Larkin & Co.

* your memo was $15,270.68
N.B. Have no further news from you, but hope soon to get Letter
& learn of your determination about travelling.

St. Louis May 4/66

Mr. M. M. Broadwell
Kansas, Mo.
Dear B.

I yesterday got yours of 27 ult[imo] & was truly surprized [sic] to learn of your going to be married, as I feared from your silence that you were sick or might be dead. I am pleased to learn of your change of life, & you have my warmest congratulation. I wish you & your beautiful little wife very many years of health, happiness & a good large house full of ch———n. Excuse me, but they will be thought about in advance. I am very slow at seeing thro' sherry[?], or I might have suspected something when you were here. You were so fatherly to Miss Wood, I did not appreciate the deeper feeling of a lover.

Well Old Fellow you have my warmest & best wishes, & I should be most happy to come up to your wedding but I have my darling little daughter Maggie at death's door with Typhoid fever, & unless she soon improves I could not well leave. As it is she is 12 Miles out in country which takes up much time. I don't think there is the least danger of any young L. [lady] declining so clever a man as yourself—& I could not advise you. If I can serve you in any way possible here, write or telegraph me.

There is no use talking *to you* about the travelling on the Plains—you are sailing elsewhere.

Hoping very soon to see you here, & with my warmest regards to all your family & Mrs. M. M. Broadwell I am Yours Very Truly,

Jas. R. Larkin

P.S. What will your pretty little wife Miss Bowne[?] say to your leaving her. Pd. $5000.00 Dft.

Above letters courtesy of Joint Collection: University of Missouri, Western Historical Manuscript Collection/Columbia State Historical Society of Missouri Manuscripts.

Notes

Chapter 1: Introduction

1. Larkin's trail inventory is included as Appendix 1.

2. Alexander Finlay and John[?] Dougherty manufactured carriages and wagons at St. Louis. While not as famous as wagon-maker Joseph Murphy of that city, Finlay & Dougherty must have produced excellent products. Their factory was located at Fifth and St. Charles, and their warehouse was at 108 North Third Street in 1854–5 (*The St. Louis Directory for the years 1854–55* [St. Louis: Chambers & Knapp, 1854], 59). In 1854 Webb & Kingsbury purchased two wagons and other goods from Finlay & Dougherty (Missouri Historical Society [hereafter referred to as MHS], Webb Collection 4–1854). The ambulance was originally a military vehicle used to transport wounded to the rear during battles. Eventually the term came to be applied to enclosed passenger wagons, often equipped with seats that folded into beds, which early travellers in the West frequently used. The conveyance is illustrated and described in Don H. Berkebile, *Car-*

riage Terminology: An Historical Dictionary (Washington, D.C.: Smithsonian Institution Press, 1978), 18.

3. James Ross Larkin's Santa Fe Trail diary of 1856–57 is now in the collections at Bent's Old Fort National Historic Site in La Junta, Colorado. Also included in the Larkin materials is a carte-de-visite with an albumin print photograph of Larkin taken about 1860, and a photocopy of a portrait of his wife, Mary Chambers Larkin. Hereafter, the Larkin Santa Fe Trail diary will be referred to as "Larkin ms. diary (1856–57)."

4. Larkin ms. diary (1856–57) contains passages concerning William Bent and the events and conditions at Bent's New Fort during November 1856. Larkin's reference to James Grey's "Roseville" establishes the existence of a Santa Fe Trail hostelry not mentioned elsewhere.

5. Compare Henry Inman, *The Old Santa Fe Trail: The Story of a Great Highway*, (New York: The MacMillan Company, 1897), Robert L. Duffus, *The Santa Fe Trail*, (New York: Longmans, Green and Co, 1930), and Seymour V. Connor and Jimmy M. Skaggs, *Broadcloth and Britches: The Santa Fe Trade*, (College Station and London: Texas A & M University Press, 1977). While factual and interpretive credibility improved over time, all three works fail to deal adequately with the 1850s, mistakenly suggesting that the dozen years between the Mexican and Civil Wars are of little interest or significance. The volume of trade during the 1850s probably was less than during war years but the decade marked the establishment of significant patterns of inter-action between native and Anglo-American that would prevail for many years. For a survey of the range of Santa Fe Trail literature, I have relied upon Jack D. Rittenhouse's *The Santa Fe Trail: A Historical Bibliography* (Albuquerque: University of New Mexico Press, 1971).

6. Among the best early primary trail accounts are "The Journals of Capt. Thomas [sic] Becknell from Boone's Lick to Santa Fe and from Santa Cruz to Green River," *Missouri Historical Review*, 4 (January 1910): 65–84; Thomas James, *Three Years Among the Indians and Mexicans* (St. Louis: Missouri Historical Society,

1916); Kate L. Gregg, ed., *The Road to Santa Fe: The Journal and Diaries of George Champlin Sibley and Others Pertaining to the Surveying and Marking of a Road from the Missouri Frontier to the Settlements of New Mexico, 1825–27* (Albuquerque: University of New Mexico Press, 1952); Josiah Gregg, *Commerce of the Prairies*, ed. by Max Moorhead (Norman: University of Oklahoma Press, 1954), and James Josiah Webb, *Adventures in the Santa Fe Trade, 1844–47*, ed. by Ralph P. Beiber. *Southwest Historical Series*, I (Glendale: Arthur H. Clark, 1931). Characteristic of works focussing on the post-1860 Indian wars is Stan Hoig, *The Sand Creek Massacre* (Norman: University of Oklahoma Press, 1961). Leo E. Oliva's excellent *Soldiers on the Santa Fe Trail* (Norman: University of Oklahoma Press, 1967) approaches the 1850s as an "era between the close of the Mexican War and the outbreak of the Civil War" (p. 93), an assumption not limited to military historians.

7. Howard R. Lamar's *The Far Southwest: 1846–1912; A Territorial History*, (New Haven: Yale University Press, 1966), the principal regional history for the territorial period, devotes twenty-five pages to the 1850s in New Mexico. Lamar's introduction refers to American territorial history as the "Dark Age of American historiography" (p. 1). Connor and Skaggs's *Broadcloth and Britches* ignores the decade altogether, and Duffus's classic, *The Santa Fe Trail*, is almost equally remiss. However, Louise Barry, *The Beginning of the West: Annals of the Kansas Gateway to the American West, 1540–1854* (Topeka: Kansas State Historical Society, 1972), Morris F. Taylor, *First Mail West: Stagecoach Lines on the Santa Fe Trail* (Albuquerque: University of New Mexico Press, 1971), Donald Chaput, *François X. Aubry: Trader, Trailmaker and Voyageur in the Southwest* (Glendale, Calif.: Arthur H. Clark Company, 1975), and Calvin Horn, *New Mexico's Troubled Years: The Story of the Early Territorial Governors* (Albuquerque: Horn & Wallace, 1964) each contain useful information for the period.

8. Alexander Majors, *Seventy Years on the Frontier: Alexander Majors' Memoirs of a Lifetime on the Border*, ed. by Prentiss In-

graham (Chicago and New York: Rand, McNally & Company, 1893); Marian Russell, *Land of Enchantment: Memoires of Marian Russell along the Santa Fe Trail;* ed. by Garnet M. Brayer, afterword by Marc Simmons (Albuquerque: University of New Mexico Press, 1981); Susan Shelby Magoffin, *Down the Santa Fe Trail and Into Mexico: The Diary of Susan Shelby Magoffin, 1846–1847,* ed. by Stella M. Drumm (New Haven: Yale University Press, 1926), and W(illiam) W(atts) H(art) Davis, *El Gringo: or, New Mexico and Her People* (New York: Harper & Brothers, 1857).

9. David Meriwether, *My Life In the Mountains and on the Plains: The Newly Discovered Autobiography of David Meriwether,* ed. by Robert A. Griffen (Norman: University of Oklahoma Press, 1965), and Franz Huning, *Trader On The Santa Fe Trail: Memoirs of Franz Huning,* with notes by Lina Fergusson Browne (Albuquerque: University of Albuquerque, 1973). The most recent addition to a list of important sources for the 1850s is David J. Weber, *Richard H. Kern: Expeditionary Artist in the Far Southwest, 1848–1853* (Albuquerque: University of New Mexico Press, 1985), which describes life in New Mexico during the early 1850s in both words and images.

Chapter 2: "In Search of Better Health"

1. Susan Ross Glasgow was born on September 29, 1811, probably at Christianna Bridge, Delaware. According to family genealogical records, James and Ann Glasgow (James Ross Larkin's maternal great-grandparents) came from Scotland during or before 1720, to settle in Delaware. They had a son, James (1717–1789), who married an Ellinor or Eleanor Stuart or Eakin, at White Clay Creek, in Newcastle, Delaware. Their marriage must have occurred very late in James' life and early in Ellinor's, for genealogical records indicate that they, too, had a son named James (1784–1856), while it is noted that Ellinor died in 1790. The third James would have been about twenty-six when he married Ann Ross at Christianna Dridge, Delaware, on July 11,

1810. Typescript copy of Larkin genealogy and family data, Folder 1–26–1875, Mullanphy Papers, MHS.

2. The Glasgow family had migrated to Missouri where Ann Ross Glasgow died at Camp Branch, Missouri, on April 17, 1819. Her daughter Susan Ross Glasgow (James Ross Larkin's mother) was soon thereafter taken to a Quaker establishment at Wilmington, Delaware, "Friend Eli Hillis' School." The school must have left a lasting and favorable impression on young Susan, for she would one day name her second son after its founder. Folder 1–26–1875 (Larkin genealogy folder), Mullanphy Papers, MHS.

3. Family tradition holds that a Thomas Larkin of Delaware, who died in 1818, was a Revolutionary War veteran who served as a "private in Captain Pope's company, Delaware Militia, 1777–78." Thomas Henry Larkin (James's father) was born on November 24, 1809, and died on July 5, 1883. Folder 1–26–1875 (Larkin genealogy folder), Mullanphy Papers, MHS.

4. The *St. Louis Globe-Democrat* noted upon the occasion of the death of Thomas H. Larkin, Jr. (James's brother), in 1901, that Thomas H. Larkin, Sr., was remembered as "a pioneer merchant of St. Louis, having been engaged in the wholesale grocery business . . . at the foot of Olive Street for many years." *St. Louis Globe-Democrat*, July 31, 1901. I have utilized Robert I. Vexler, compiler, *St. Louis: A Chronological and Documentary History, 1762–1970* for background information in this section, and in the section comparing St. Louis and Santa Fe in the 1850s, below. Calvin Horn, *New Mexico's Troubled Years: The Story of the Early Territorial Governors*, 36–49, has a brief biography of William Carr Lane.

5. Letterpress printed broadside or circular signed by Thomas H. Larkin in Missouri Historical Society in which he discusses the importance of hemp as a staple crop. Folder 1–26–1875 (Larkin genealogy folder), Mullanphy Papers, MHS. Advertisements in the *St. Louis Daily Missouri Democrat* also indicate that Larkin maintained a steady interest in the hemp market.

6. A single receipt survives from Thos. H. Larkin & Co., of

"No. 30 Levee, Corner of Olive Street," for April 8, 1857, on which date the famed Santa Fe firm of Webb & Kingsbury purchased four kegs of butter, and paid extra for additional iron hoops to be put on each keg, perhaps so they could withstand the rigorous wagon voyage out to New Mexico. Folder 4–1857 to 5–1857, Webb Collection, MHS. Also, in 1843 William Sublette had purchased three kegs of DuPont's gunpowder from Thomas H. Larkin & Company to be taken to California. Folder 1843, Sublette Papers, MHS.

7. In 1841, Thomas H. Larkin purchased a "lot . . . situated on the North West corner of Fifth & Chesnut; Block 005," from which he would ultimately realize an annual income of about $9,000.00 Probated Will of Thomas H. Larkin, file number 14,758, Probate Court Files Room, St. Louis, Missouri. Thomas H. Larkin's estate was valued variously at $142,000 to $350,000, though the latter figure seems more realistic.

8. His total personal estate at death (July 5, 1883) was valued at nearly $150,000.00 by the court of the City of St. Louis, of which James's family seem to have received about $10,000. Probated Will of Thomas H. Larkin, file number 14,758, Probate Court Files Room, St. Louis, Missouri. Additional financial information emerges from city census records for 1859 and 1860. These indicate that Thomas H. Larkin owned real estate in 1850 valued at $15,000, while James, aged 19, owned no real estate and lived at his parent's home, employed as a clerk. By 1860, James no longer lived at his parents' home, and was listed as a "merchant," married to Mary. He owned $40,000 worth of real estate and $4,000 in personal wealth. His father by that time owned $108,000 in real estate and $81,000 in personal wealth. In addition, Thomas H. Larkin supported his wife and five children, a middle-aged relative, and five servants, one of whom was black. St. Louis City Census for 1850, Ward 3, p. 370; 1860 Census, Ward 6, pp. 437, 462.

9. Eli Hilles Larkin studied chemistry in St. Louis as well as in Germany and Austria and, with Henry W. Scheffer, originated the firm of "Larkin & Scheffer, Manufacturing Chemists." Even-

tually, the firm was incorporated as the "Larkin & Scheffer Chemical Company," and continued until purchased in 1890 by the National Ammonia Company. In 1879, Larkin & Scheffer received credit for developing the "commercial manufacture of liquid anhydrous ammonia." In addition, E. H. Larkin "designed the first anhydrous ammonia shipping cylinder, which has made possible the operation of isolated ammonia-type ice making and refrigerating plants throughout the world." Described as a philanthropist millionaire, Eli Hilles Larkin's stellar career as a chemist reflects an outstanding education as well as sound business acumen. In a eulogistic pamphlet, he was described as "generous even to a fault . . . modest and retiring always." Eli Hilles Larkin is said to have donated nearly one-half million dollars to charitable organizations, notably the St. Louis Children's Hospital and The David Rankin, Jr. School of Mechanical Trades, also in St. Louis. A contemporary newspaper account, however, gives the reduced figure of $45,000.00 as his bequest to the hospital. In addition, it seems there was a scandal that attended Hilles's death. Eli Hilles Larkin, the "millionaire chemist and philanthropist," was a bachelor whose private life was a closed book, even to his business associates. But soon after his death at the age of eighty-one it was revealed that he had lived for many years with Harriet B. Thompson. He had seemingly posed as her husband and they dwelled together in a home on fashionable Forest Park Boulevard. E. H. Larkin's niece, Mrs. C. C. Cummings, told a reporter that her uncle had died of a broken heart following the death of Miss Thompson. *St. Louis Globe-Democrat,* August 11, 1920; and "Brief Notes on the life of the late Eli Hilles Larkin," St. Louis, Mo., May 6, 1920, in Mullanphy Papers, MHS.

10. Folder 1–30–1843, William Carr Lane Collection, MHS. On the occasion of little Annie's death, William Carr Lane, later to become the second territorial governor of New Mexico (1852–53), wrote to Mary E. Lane, of Terre Haute, Indiana, that Mrs. Larkin's "grief was agonizing but perfectly silent. These Glasgows are a peculiar people—they are so quiet and submissive. I believe Mrs. Larkin has joined the Unitarian Communion, since the

death of Annie." Folder 2–23–1843, Lane Collection, MHS. See also Horn, *New Mexico's Troubled Years,* 36–51.

11. Margaret Lewis Foote Larkin had married a William Holmes Thomson on July 16, 1862, and gave birth to a daughter on April 2, 1863, two weeks before she died, on April 15, 1863, presumably of complications resulting from her daughter's birth. William H. Thomson later became the president of the prestigious Boatman's Bank of St. Louis. Folder 1–26–1875, Mullanphy Papers, MHS.

12. Susan Larkin was born in 1851 and died in 1907. Folder 1–26–1875 (Larkin genealogy), Mullanphy Papers, MHS. During 1860, the Larkin daughters spent the summer at Jefferson Kearny Clark's country home, Minoma, near St. Louis. Other references are found in Francis Hurd Stadler, "Letters From Minoma," 237–59; Charles van Ravensway, "Years of Turmoil, Years of Growth: St. Louis in the 1850's," 303–24, and William G. B. Carson, "Secesh," 119–45.

13. Mary Cuthbert Larkin was born on July 19, 1844, and lived until 1910. During the Civil War, in 1862, her plans to marry David Lynn Magruder caused unrest among her family, most of whom had secessionist leanings. Her husband-to-be, D. L. Magruder, had joined the army in New Mexico, in August 1850, and was stationed that year at Taos and Rayado, New Mexico. He was still in New Mexico, although at Santa Fe in 1856, when Larkin met him, presumably for the first time. While on an official army tour of inspection of personnel and installations in New Mexico during 1850, Col. George Archibald McCall noted that Magruder filled a valuable position, "there being no army medical officer at Taos, nor any practicing [sic] physician in the town." Col. George Archibald McCall, *New Mexico In 1850: A Military View,* ed., Robert W. Frazer, 145, 147, 194; Carson, "Secesh," 122, 122n.; Folder 1–26–1875 (Larkin genealogy), Mullanphy Papers, MHS.

14. Larkin ms. diary (1856–57) refers to a partnership with his father on December 31, 1856, p. 90.

15. Letters from Larkin to Broadwell are included as Appendix 3. Letters courtesy of Joint Collection: University of Missouri, Western Historical Manuscript Collection/ Columbia State Historical Society of Missouri Manuscripts.

16. James Ross Larkin diaries for 1869 and 1874, Mullanphy Papers, MHS, indicate that he is almost always at home. He comments on family matters, visitors, rent collection, and socializing, but never on market conditions or events at the workplace. See also the note book containing plats and accounts in Larkin folder, Mullanphy Papers, MHS. The Larkin family held large tracts of city real estate, and even leased entire blocks to business in the city, as well as retaining ownership of numerous houses rented to residents of St. Louis. During the late 1860s and early 1870s, James kept a separate day book that contained nothing but dozens of notations concerning house plats and income derived from their rental. Larkin lived with his family in or near downtown St. Louis until his marriage. The family residence between 1851 and 1855 is listed as the "northwest corner of 5th and Chesnut," but in 1853–54 James's occupation and residence is listed as "clerk, 53 Levee, between Locust and Vine." During 1857, he "boarded" at the "corner of 5th and Chesnut," and seems to have remained there until 1859. In 1864 James lived at 216 O'Fallon, moving once more by 1868 to 1418 O'Fallon, then in 1870 to 1405 O'Fallon, where he dwelled until his death in 1874. *The St. Louis City Directory For The Years 1854–5* (St. Louis: Chambers & Knapp, 1854); also *St. Louis City Directories for 1857, 1859, 1860, 1864, 1868, 1870, 1874.*

17. Larkin ms. diary (1856–57), 7, 41, 80, 97.

18. Carte-de-visite in Bent's Old Fort N.H.S. Larkin materials.

19. Mary Chambers was born on July 17, 1833, at the home of her parents at Tailles des Noyers, "amid the forest primeval, situated on a hill commanding a view of the beautiful Florissant Valley." The Chambers family also built Dunmore Cottage, outside the city, where Mary's mother lived during her last years, and at which the Larkins were frequent visitors. Mary received a

Catholic education at schools such as the Ladies of the Sacred Heart in Florissant, the Sisters of Loretto in St. Louis, and the Visitation Academy at Kaskaskia, Illinois. She died on August 7, 1918. *St. Louis Globe Democrat,* August 16, 1918; Larkin ms. diaries for 1869 and 1874, Mullanphy Papers; and a portrait of Mary Chambers in the Missouri Historical Society Pictorial History collections.

20. Ruth K. Field, "Some Misconceptions About Lucas Place," 122, n.2 (plate 2 shows a fine photograph of the Larkin mansion); also *St. Louis City Directory for 1860.*

21. *St. Louis Globe-Democrat,* August 16, 1918, and Larkin ms. diary (1856–57), 75, 78.

22. Larkin ms. diary (1856–57), 106

23. Larkin ms. diary for 1869, date of June 8, and also 1869 entry listing income in folder 1–26–1875 (Larkin genealogy), Mullanphy Papers, MHS.

24. Letters of April 11, 16, 18, May 4, 1866 from James Ross Larkin to W. W. Broadwell, of Kansas City, concerning a planned prairie trip are transcribed in Appendix 3. Joint Collection, University of Missouri/State Historical Society, Columbia, Missouri. See also Larkin ms. diary (1856–57), 106.

25. Larkin ms. diary (1856–57), 106–07.

26. Lost in the fire were "articles of the Larkin family stored in a room on the second floor. . . . These were said to consist of family portraits and furniture representative of the best of the period when the house was built and before. . . . Several pieces of French period furniture, including a mahogany Napoleon bed, were among the pieces of furniture destroyed." *St. Louis Globe-Democrat,* August 16, 1918; *St. Louis Globe-Democrat,* April 21, 1937. Copies of portraits of James and Mary Larkin survive in the Missouri Historical Society Pictorial History collection.

27. *St. Louis Globe-Democrat,* August 16, 1918. See also National Park Service, Bent's Old Fort N.H.S. museum accession number 184, dated 1979, for documents relating to the gift of the diary to the NPS.

Chapter 3: St. Louis and Santa Fe

1. *St. Louis Daily Missouri Democrat,* September 19, 1856. The preponderance of German speakers in St. Louis would account for James Ross Larkin's familiarity with the language.

2. This sketch of St. Louis is based on Richard C. Wade, *The Urban Frontier: The Rise of Western Cities, 1790–1830* (Cambridge: Harvard University Press, 1959); Howard R. Lamar, *The Reader's Encyclopedia of the American West;* van Ravenswaay, "Years of Turmoil, Years of Growth: St. Louis in the 1850s," 303–24, and two contemporary newspapers, the *St. Louis Missouri Republican* and the *St. Louis Missouri Daily Democrat.*

3. Wade, *The Urban Frontier,* 63–64.

4. *St. Louis Daily Missouri Democrat,* March 12, 1857, p. 2.

5. *Ibid.*

6. Stanley Sadie, ed. *The New Grove Dictionary of Music and Musicians* (20 vols., London: MacMillan Publishing, 1980), 18: 723.

7. William Clark Kennerly (as told to Elizabeth Russell), *Persimmon Hill: A Narrative of Old St. Louis and the Far West,* 96–97.

8. James's sisters, Mary and Margaret Larkin, spent the summer at Jefferson Kearny Clark's country home, Minoma, in 1860. Stadler, "Letters From Minoma," 16, 247n.

9. *St. Louis Missouri Republican,* September 15, 1856, p. 2. Under the heading "From Kansas," the report indicates that the *Morning Star* arrived on the 14th from St. Joseph bringing news of trouble in Kansas. Among James's relatives, only William Henry Glasgow, Jr., seems to have been an ardent abolitionist; the remainder of the family generally supported the Southern position. Stadler, "Letters From Minoma," 237–59.

10. *St. Louis Daily Missouri Democrat,* September 23, 1856, p. 2.

11. B. M. Lynch ran advertisements in the *St. Louis Daily Missouri Democrat,* and in the *St. Louis Missouri Republican,* from March to June 1857, and presumably at other times.

12. *St. Louis Daily Missouri Democrat*, March 13, 1857, p. 1.

13. Josiah Gregg, Marian Russell, and others were "enchanted" by the trail, and claimed they loved trail life more than anything else. Therefore, one might say that the trail attracted travellers because of its aesthetic qualities, as well as for pecuniary reasons. For examples see Josiah Gregg, *Commerce of the Prairies: or the Journal of a Santa Fe Trader*, 328–29, and Marian Russell, *Land of Enchantment: Memoires of Marian Russell along the Santa Fe Trail*, 93.

14. Robert M. Utley, "Fort Union and the Santa Fe Trail," 36–48; Chris Emmett, *Fort Union and the Winning of the Southwest*.

15. Houghton's contracts to build a state house and penitentiary grossed about $150,000 over a seven-year period. Howard R. Lamar, *The Far Southwest: 1846–1912; A Territorial History*, 90–91.

16. *Santa Fe Weekly Gazette*, October 25, 1856.

17. Russell, *Land of Enchantment*, and Stella M. Drumm, ed. *Down the Santa Fe Trail and into Mexico, the Diary of Susan Shelby Magoffin; 1846–1847*.

18. Lamar, *The Far Southwest*, pp. 56–108.

19. Lamar, *The Far Southwest*, 107–8, and Ralph Emerson Twitchell, *The Leading Facts of New Mexican History*, 2: 291–326.

Chapter 4: The Health Frontier

1. Billy M. Jones, *Health-Seekers In The Southwest, 1817–1900*, 39–40 summarizes the work of Doctor Daniel Drake, who published in 1850 *A Systematic Treatise, Historical, Etiological, and Practical on the Principal Diseases of the Interior Valley of North America* (Cincinnati: Winthrop B. Smith, 1850). Also available were Gregg's *Commerce of the Prairies* (1844), Matt Field's 1839–41 newspaper articles printed in the New Orleans *Picayune*, the St. Louis *Reveille* and other papers [reprinted as *Matt Field on the Santa Fe Trail*, collected by Clyde and Mae Reed Porter, John E. Sunder, ed. (Norman: University of Oklahoma Press, 1960)], George Catlin's *Letters and Notes on the Manners, Customs and*

Conditions of the North American Indians (New York: Wiley and Putnam, 1841), and George Douglas Brewerton's "Incidents of Travel in New Mexico," *Harper's New Monthly Magazine*, 8 (April 1854), 577–96. Interestingly, James Larkin seems to have been a regular reader of this journal.

2. For a summary of this development, see Jones, *Health-Seekers*, 88 ff.

3. Native Americans, it is generally acknowledged, suffered population losses due to disease—principally imported from Europe—on the order of 90 percent. The same prairie that served as a health haven for Caucasians became the scene of dismal suffering for its original tenants, a factor that Jones fails to address in his *Health-Seekers*. Because fewer travellers went on the Santa Fe Trail than on the Oregon-California trail (said to be littered with graves), outbreaks of cholera and other deadly diseases posed less of a threat.

4. John E. Baur, "The Health Seeker in the Westward Movement, 1830–1900," 92.

5. The Sublette brothers, Robert Campbell, and Charles Larpenteur all improved while in the plains or Rockies. Jones, *Health-Seekers*, 53. Kennerly, *Persimmon Hill*, 143–67, has a chapter about wealthy health seekers from St. Louis who traveled in the Rocky Mountain West in 1843 with Sir William Drummond Stewart.

6. Baur, "The Health Seeker in the Westward Movement, 1830–1900," 92–93; and Gregg, *Commerce of the Prairies*, 223.

7. Gregg, *Commerce of the Prairies*, 23.

8. Folders 7–18–1840, 8–11–(1844?) [sic], Lane Collection, MHS, and a letter sent in 1858 by Susan Glasgow Larkin, of St. Louis, to Sarah L. Glasgow, in Arkansas, folder 12–17–1858, Lane Collection, MHS.

9. At least three such letters are included in the Webb Collection of the MHS archives at St. Louis, listed as 6–5–1855, 5–31–1856, and 9–17–1856, the latter being that given to Larkin. Also mentioned are George Collier, of St. Louis, and W. W. Shaw, of New Orleans.

10. *The Encyclopaedia Britannica,* 9th edition (New York: Charles Scribner's Sons, 1882), "Neuralgia," 17: 363–64.

11. In 1870, Susan Glasgow Larkin wrote to William Glasgow, Jr., about her concern for Sarah L. Glasgow, who frequently injected morphine under her skin, as indicated in folder 7–27–1870? [sic], Lane Collection, MHS.

12. See *Santa Fe Weekly Gazette* article of July 11, 1857, reprinted in Appendix 2.

Chapter 5: The Trail to Santa Fe

1. Baur, "The Health Seeker in the Westward Movement, 1830–1900," 91–110; Peter D. Olch, "Treading the Elephant's Tail: Medical Problems on the Overland Trails," 196–212; and Frederick A. Wislizenus, *Memoir of a Tour to Northern Mexico, Connected With Col. Doniphan's Expedition, in 1846 and 1847.*

2. Howard R. Lamar, "Rites of Passage: Young Men and Their Families in the Overland Trails Experience, 1843–69," *"Soul Butter and Hog Wash," and Other Essays on the American West,* Thomas G. Alexander, ed., (Provo: Brigham Young University Press, 1978), 33–67.

3. Lamar, "Rites of Passage," 35.

4. Gregg, *Commerce of the Prairies,* 30–32.

5. Ingraham, *Seventy Years On The Frontier,* 71–73.

6. Larkin ms. diary (1856–57), 40–43, has passages that record Bent's reaction to illegal whiskey trading at his fort.

7. Lamar, "Rites of Passage," 39.

8. Lamar, "Rites of Passage," 44.

9. Larkin ms. diary (1856–57), 42–43, 90.

10. Larkin ms. diary (1856–57), 18–19.

11. Larkin ms. diary (1856–57), 29–30. George Bent's account of his father's New Fort does not include the episode witnessed by Larkin. George was at the time under the guardianship of A. G. Boone or W. R. Bernard, at Westport. William had sent his son there to be educated in 1853, and George did not return to the

plains for a decade. George E. Hyde, *Life of George Bent Written From His Letters*, 94–105.

12. Larkin ms. diary (1856–57), 40–41.

13. Nolie Mumey, *Old Forts And Trading Posts of the West: Bent's Old Fort and Bent's New Fort on the Arkansas River*, 133 ff. William Bent's letter of August 25, 1856, is reproduced on page 137.

14. Larkin ms. diary (1856–57), 37, 50.

15. Larkin ms. diary (1856–57), 59.

16. DeWitt C. Peters, *The Life and Adventures of Kit Carson, The Nestor of The Rocky Mountains.*

17. Larkin ms. diary (1856–57), 66.

18. *Santa Fe Weekly Gazette*, October 25, 1856, p. 2. Jean François Pinard had indeed been an officer in the French military, but was ordained in France and came to New Mexico with Bishop Jean Baptiste Lamy. He served as pastor at Las Vegas from 1853 until at least 1858. J. B. Salpointe, *Soldiers of the Cross, Notes on the Ecclesiastical History of New Mexico, Arizona and Colorado*, 218.

19. John L. Kessell, *Kiva, Cross and Crown: The Pecos Indians and New Mexico 1540–1840*, 459–63.

20. Larkin ms. diary (1856–57), 71, 90.

21. Larkin ms. diary (1856–57), 72.

22. Larkin ms. diary (1856–57), 72–75, 95–96.

23. *Santa Fe Weekly Gazette*, July 11, 1857, p. 2, has an article, "Arrivals From The States," mentioning that Larkin recently arrived at that city, indicating that he had probably made a second round trip in 1857, before returning once again to St. Louis. The article is reproduced in Appendix 2.

24. Letters from Larkin to M. M. Broadwell of Kansas City, Missouri, discussing the planned trip are reproduced in Appendix 3.

Annotation to the Larkin Diary

1. Cape May: New Jersey coast; Catskill Mts.: New York resort region; Nahant: Essex County, Massachusetts, about nine miles northeast of Boston on the seashore. Rockbridge and Alum Springs: Rockbridge County, Virginia, is on the crest of the Shenandoah Mountains in a region of numerous hot springs. There is a White Sulpher Springs in nearby Greenbriar County, West Virginia, formerly a summer resort for presidents Martin Van Buren, John Tyler and Millard Fillmore. These sites were among the nineteenth century's leading health resorts. Although he had relatives at Cape May and perhaps in Virginia, health touring certainly would have been costly, and Larkin's trip to the east in 1856 must have taken several weeks. An article copied from a Philadelphia newspaper appeared in the *St. Louis Missouri Republican* noting that the Mount Vernon Hotel, a 432-room resort hotel at Cape May, had burned to the ground. Perhaps Larkin had dined in one of the many restaurants and bars within the gigantic wooden Victorian hotel. *St. Louis Missouri Republican*, September 13, 1856, p. 2.

2. Mr. Wm Bent: William W. Bent (1809–1869), with broth-

ers Charles, George, and Robert, and Ceran St. Vrain, organized in about 1830 the firm of Bent, St. Vrain & Co., to engage in the fur trade and the Indian and Mexican trades of the southern plains. By 1856 William Bent had five growing children, and had lived among the Cheyennes for better than two decades. William Bent's name appears frequently in the Santa Fe and St. Louis newspapers, and would have been familiar to thousands of readers. Since about 1853, he had contracted to freight Cheyenne annuity goods to Bent's New Fort. He also made at least one trip each year to Westport or St. Louis to acquire goods for his own trade with the Indians, and to visit his old friends A. G. Boone and W. R. Bernard and his farm at Westport. Samuel P. Arnold, "William W. Bent," LeRoy R. Hafen, ed., *Mountain Men and the Fur Trade*, 6: 61–84; David Lavender, *Bent's Fort*, especially 323–34. On September 13, 1856, the *St. Louis Missouri Republican* carried a notice that "Bent's train of wagons from New Mexico" had arrived at Westport unmolested by Kansas insurgents.

3. Bent's Fort: The reference here is to Bent's New Fort, built in 1853. Mumey, *Bent's Old Fort and Bent's New Fort on the Arkansas River*; Lavender, *Bent's Fort*.

4. 550 miles: Surveyor George C. Sibley in 1825 found the entire trail, from Fort Osage in Missouri to Santa Fe, to be about· 812 miles. Josiah Gregg noted the distance from Independence to Santa Fe to be 775 miles. In 1853, Gwin Harris Heap found Bent's Old Fort to be 547 miles from Westport, and Bent's New Fort is about thirty-five miles east of the Old Fort. Gregg, ed., *The Road to Santa Fe*, 211; Barry, *The Beginning of the West*, 1018; Gregg, *Commerce of the Prairies*, 217, n.4.

5. Westport: Westport was incorporated in April 1834 and would supplant Franklin and Independence, Missouri, as a debarkation point for Santa Fe. Westport would remain the principal outfitting point for the Santa Fe Trail, while St. Joseph served that purpose for the overland trails. Westport Landing was four miles north of Westport proper. Larkin's "Kansas" is the community that grew around and eventually engulfed Westport Landing. Barry, *The Beginning of the West*, 261, and Marc Simmons, *Follow-*

ing the Santa Fe Trail, 50–62. For the early development and significance of Westport, see William R. Bernard, "Westport and the Santa Fe Trade," 552–65. An illustration of Westport Landing as it would have appeared when Larkin stepped off the *Morning Star* is in Simmons, *Following the Santa Fe Trail,* 52.

6. Wm Glasgow: James Ross Larkin's cousins, William Henry and Edward James Glasgow, were leading merchants in St. Louis. Related through James's mother, the Glasgow brothers helped James orchestrate his Santa Fe Trail venture. See section on Larkin's biography, above.

7. Pacific R.R.: The Missouri Pacific Rail Road, chartered in 1849, was organized on January 31, 1850, at St. Louis with eleven stockholders subscribing to $154,000 of stock. Road building commenced in 1851, and by March 1, 1856, the line reached Jefferson City, a total of 125 miles. "At this point, connections were made with a daily line of steamboats for Kansas City, Leavenworth, and other Missouri River points. On account of the financial crises of 1857, but little building was done beyond Jefferson City, only twenty-five miles additional being finished up to the end of March, 1858. At this date, the earnings of the road averaged for the year $5,346 per mile." R. J. Compton, ed., *Pictorial St. Louis; A Topographical Survey Drawn in Perspective,* 1875, 146–47; John D. Cruise, "Early Days on the Union Pacific," 529–49.

8. "Morning Star": The sidewheel steamboat of 465 tons measured 227' by 34' and was built in 1856 at Elizabeth, Pennsylvania, at a cost to Captain Thomas H. Brierly of $45,000. "No more elegant steamer ever floated on the Missouri River, if indeed, on any Western river. . . . The excellence of her table is spoken of to this day, and the style of her waiters, who wore evening suits when serving dinner, including white gloves with stars on the gauntlets." The vessel, a "lower-river passenger packet," operated from 1856 to 1859, when she burned at "Bissell's point, on the Mississippi, just above St. Louis, when laid up for the winter." Albert R. Greene, "The Kansas River—Its Navigation," 319, 337, 345–6; and Phil. E. Chappell, "A History of the Missouri

River," 287, 307, 583. No known photograph exists of this vessel, but a representative type is illustrated on page 292, ibid. Advertisements for "Season Arrangements" for the *Morning Star* and other steamers appeared daily in St. Louis newspapers, for example the *St. Louis Daily Missouri Democrat* for July 23, 1856. E. W. Gould, *Fifty Years on the Mississippi; Or, Gould's History of River Navigation* (St. Louis: Nixon-Jones Printing Company, 1889), 416–17. Thomas Brierly was "one of the most popular and well-known captains on the river, and commanded several boats, among them the Ben W. Lewis, El Paso, Morning Star, F. X. Aubrey, and the famous James H. Lucas." "Errata and Addenda," *Transactions of the Kansas State Historical Society, 1905–1906*, 9: 583, n. 319. In 1858 Brierly, Captain Samuel Burke, and ten other captains formed the "St. Louis and St. Joseph Union Packet Line" in response to a need for improved scheduling and safer operation of steamer traffic on the Missouri River. The vast migration beginning in 1849 to California, and later, to Kansas, Iowa, and Nebraska, "induced boat owners to take great risks and to add large numbers of new boats to the trade." But the effort failed due to "the shortness of the navigation season and the dangers of navigation, together with the long distance over such precarious navigation." The dangers inherent in river traffic were obviously great, for all twelve boats in the concern were lost within a few years. Gould, *Fifty Years on the Mississippi*, 416–17.

9. Penitentiary: "In 1836 the state of Missouri built a penitentiary at Jefferson City at a cost of $25,000.00. The penitentiary consisted of several small buildings with accommodations for forty prisoners located on four acres of land and enclosed by a wooden stockade." Duane Meyer, *The Heritage of Missouri: A History*, (St. Louis: State Publishing Company, 1963), 163.

10. Brunswick: A small town on the north bank of the Missouri River in present Chariton county, Missouri. It was formerly important as a depot for the trade to the Grand River area in Kansas. Located on "Keemle Wetmore's map of Missouri, 1837, the town of Brunswick is placed on a sharp northern bend of the river." In 1858, Brunswick still was on the river's bank, but by 1905, the

channel of the Missouri had moved five miles away. Chappell, "A History of the Missouri River," 269, n. 129.

11. Miami and Waverly: Small towns on the south bank of the Missouri River in present Lafayette county, Missouri.

12. Lexington: Inaugurated in 1822, Lexington was the headquarters for two important firms connected with the Santa Fe trade: the Aull brothers, and Russell, Majors and Waddell. Simmons, *Following the Santa Fe Trail,* 31–33.

13. Kansas troubles: Here Larkin refers to the growing sectional dispute over the slavery issue centered in the newly organized territories of Kansas and Nebraska, created by an act of congress in May 1854. "Bleeding Kansas" would remain a focus of national and regional interest until 1858. It contributed significantly to the rise of the Republican party in 1856, and subsequent polarization throughout the nation, but perhaps especially in Missouri and other border states. The rush of Free Soilers and proslavery men into the territory provided a boost to St. Louis businessmen, who sold weapons and supplies to both factions.

14. Mr. Hays: Seth M. Hayes resided at Westport, Missouri, at least as early as 1839 and is probably indicated here. In the mid-1840s Hayes worked as a trader for Frederick Chouteau near the Kansas Methodist Mission. In April 1847, Seth M. Hayes (a bachelor) was placed in charge of the first trading house at Council Grove (Morris County, Ks.), owned by the Westport firm of (Albert G.) Boone & (James G.) Hamilton. An Army blacksmith shop established there in August 1846 still operated the following year. Seth Hayes is reported to have resided and worked at Council Grove until at least 1860. Consult index listing for Seth Hayes in Barry, *The Beginning of the West;* Cruise, "Early Days on the Union Pacific," 533.

15. Messrs. Bernard: William R. Bernard and a brother, James[?], ran an outfitting and mercantile business at Westport well known to travellers on the Santa Fe Trail. J. & W. R. Bernard succeeded Kearney & Bernard, also of Westport. In 1853 Charles E. Kearney and Bernard formed an outfitting business, and two years later Kearney & Bernard would outfit 1,217 wag-

ons. Barry, *The Beginning of the West*, 1210. W. R. Bernard was born in 1823 in Albemarle county, Virginia, and lived until at least 1905. He worked variously as a farmer, miner, and government geologist, until he settled at Westport in 1848. His sister, name unknown, married a J. G. Hamilton (see below), also in business at Westport, and his visit to her in 1847 may have resulted in Bernard's decision to remain at Westport. Bernard was well acquainted with Kit Carson, William Bent, Lucien B. Maxwell, François X. Aubrey, Senator Thomas Hart Benton, and many other prominent figures of the Missouri frontier. He engaged in business at Westport in 1848 with Col. A. G. Boone. Boone & Bernard is said to have been instrumental in drawing the Santa Fe trade from Independence to Westport and also engaged in the Indian trade with the Kansas, Sacs, and Foxes in 1850, with the Osages in 1851, and with the Pottawatomies in 1852. Barry, *The Beginning of the West*, 897, 1059. William R. Bernard was the guardian of one of William Bent's children, Charles, who "was under the care of Bernard until the close of the civil war, when he left for the plains, and became one of the most cruel of Indian warriors that ever scourged the Santa Fe trail." Bernard, "Westport and the Santa Fe Trade," 564.

16. Mr. Hamilton: This may be J. G. Hamilton, a merchant of Westport mentioned by Bernard, "Westport and the Santa Fe Trade," 564.

17. Indian Creek: In present Johnson county, Kansas, slightly west of the Missouri state line and about twelve miles from Westport. Gwin Harris Heap noted in 1854 that Indian Creek was abundantly supplied with cottonwoods, willows, and grass. Barry, *The Beginning of the West*, 1018, 1153.

18. Bull's Creek: In Johnson county, Kansas, about thirty-five miles from Westport, Missouri. Gwin Harris Heap noted "some timber; good grass and water" in 1853. A few Shawnee cabins were also nearby. Barry, *The Beginning of the West*, 1018, 1152.

19. Mr. Allison: William Allison, among other activities, received mail contracts for Santa Fe, Fort Laramie, and Salt Lake between 1851 and 1854. See entries under "William Allison" in

Barry, *The Beginning of the West*. LeRoy and Ann Hafen quote from David Kellogg in 1857: "Bill Allison, a one-armed plains-man, has a stockade [at Allison's ranch] and trades with the Indians." LeRoy R. Hafen and Ann W. Hafen, eds., *Relations with the Indians of the Plains, 1857–1861: A Documentary Account of the Military Campaigns, and Negotiations of Indian Agents—with Re-ports and Journals of P. G. Lowe, R. M. Peck, J. E. B. Stuart, S. D. Sturgis, and Other Official Papers*, volume 9 of *The Far West and the Rockies Historical Series* 15 vols. (Glendale: Arthur H. Clark Company, 1959), 103, n. 8. The editors refer to "Across the Plains in 1858, Diary of Daniel [David] Kellogg," in the *Trail* (n.d.) 5:7.

20. Walnut Creek: Walnut Creek enters the Arkansas River near Great Bend, Kansas, where Allison's ranch was located. One writer noted in 1859 that the ranch was "built of Poles inclosed with Sod. The roof is nearly flat one story high. The Stone Walls and Sods inclose about an Acre of Land. This affords a strong protection against Indians. Here is a Mail Station, Store, Tavern, Corn & Hay, etc." Hafen and Hafen, *Relations with the Indians of the Plains*, 103, n. 8.

21. Willow Spring: A few miles east of present Overbrook, Kansas, in Douglas County. Simmons, *Following the Santa Fe Trail*, 76–77. For modern illustrations of some of the historic sites on the trail see the photographs in Marc Simmons and Joan Myers, *Along the Santa Fe Trail*.

22. Lawrence: Headquarters of the free soilers and the Em-migrant Aid Company in Kansas and the site of many distur-bances during the "Bleeding Kansas" episodes. It suffered attacks by pro-slavery men in May and September 1856. For a contempo-rary description by a Santa Fe Trail traveller in 1858, see H. B. Möllhausen, "Over the Santa Fe Trail Through Kansas in 1858," 376.

23. Hundred & Ten Creek: Famous camping place on the Santa Fe Trail located between Overbrook and Scranton, Kansas, one hundred and ten miles from Fort Osage on the Missouri River. Possibly the "ruffians" to whom James alludes hung about

the McGee-Harris stage station that had been at 110 Mile Creek since 1854. Simmons, *Following the Santa Fe Trail*, 78–79, and Hobart E. Stocking, *The Road To Santa Fe* 75–77.

24. Soldier Creek: In Osage or Shawnee County, Kansas.

25. Prairie City: A free-soiler settlement in Franklin County, Kansas, near present Baldwin. For a contemporary account of the conflicts that took place there during autumn 1856 see G. W. E. Griffith, "The Battle of Black Jack," 524–28.

26. Mr. Bent's Lady: The daughter of Southern Cheyenne tribal leader Grey Thunder, Yellow Woman (18??–1865) was the sister of Owl Woman, Bent's first wife with whom he had lived since 1837. Owl Woman bore William four children and died giving birth to Charles in 1847. As was customary among the Cheyennes, William then took for his wife Yellow Woman, with whom he and Owl Woman had lived for many years. Owl Woman, who in 1849 bore a daughter, Julia, was killed by Pawnee scouts working for the army in 1865. Arnold, "William W. Bent," 61–84. "Evidently Yellow Woman frequently visited the [Bent's] Westport farm, something her elder sister seems to have done but rarely." Lavender, *Bent's Fort*, 323.

27. 142 [Mile Creek]: A tributary of the Kansas River, in Lyon County, Kansas, one hundred and forty-two miles from Fort Osage.

28. Council Grove: The most renowned campsite on the eastern part of the Santa Fe Trail, located in present Morris County on the Neosho River bottom. First named in 1825 by George Champlin Sibley, Council Grove was the westernmost stand of hardwood timber available for spare wagon axles. Small trains would gather here to form huge caravans under quasi-military order for protection from Plains Indian raiders. For the best contemporary account see Gregg's *Commerce of the Prairies*, 29–36.

29. Kaw Indians: The Kaw or Kansas tribe were Siouan speakers who lived near Council Grove (1846–73) during the time of Larkin's trip. A few Methodist missions were established between 1850 and 1854 near the grove, but the Kansas resisted efforts at

Christianization. In the winter of 1852–53 smallpox killed about one-quarter of the approximately 1,700 who lived at Council Grove. By the time Larkin saw the tribe, they had been reduced to a deplorable condition. Frederick Webb Hodge, ed., *The Handbook of American Indians North of Mexico*, Bureau of American Ethnology, Bulletin 30 (Washington: Government Printing Office, 1906) 1: 653–55.

30. Diamond Spring: Diamond Spring is in Morris County, Kansas. George Champlin Sibley in 1825 named the spring "Diamond of the Plain" after a similarly named Arabian oasis and spring, the "Diamond of the Desert." In 1849, Waldo, Hall & Company built a stage station at the spring. Gregg, *Commerce of the Prairies*, 36; "Explanation of Map," *KHC* 9 (1905–06), 571; Simmons, *Following the Santa Fe Trail*, 87–88.

31. Majors & Russell: Alexander Majors and William Russell operated the largest freighting concern on the Santa Fe Trail. Larkin fails to note if either of the principals accompanied the train he encountered. Between 1855 and spring 1858 the firm was styled Majors & Russell. The best accounts of this firm are Henry Pickering Walker, *The Wagonmasters*, and Ingraham, *Seventy Years On The Frontier*.

32. Dr. H. Connelly: Henry Connelly (1800–1866) was a native of Kentucky. He practiced medicine briefly in Missouri before joining a Santa Fe Trail caravan in 1828. In 1846, Connelly, with James Magoffin, helped ease the American takeover of New Mexico, and by 1856 he had risen to prominence in Santa Fe while serving as territorial counselor from Bernalillo County between 1853 and 1859. President Abraham Lincoln appointed him territorial governor in 1861, and again in 1864, and Connelly managed to keep the territory in the union. Horn, *New Mexico's Troubled Years*, 93–113.

33. Santa Fe Mail Company: Waldo, Hall and Company began the monthly Independence-to-Santa Fe mail and passenger service in 1850 and continued until 1857, when the firm became Hockaday and Hall. Among other functions, the mail stage car-

ried newspapers between Santa Fe and St. Louis. The most thorough account of the early mail service on the Santa Fe Trail is Taylor, *First Mail West.*

34. Cottonwood Creek: Hobart E. Stocking notes that wagons travelled as far as Council Grove "singly or in small groups. Beyond they travelled as a unit, generally in a single column, to Cottonwood Creek in the vicinity of Durham, Kansas. West of that crossing they travelled in two parallel columns to about Walnut Creek draining into the Arkansas River at its Great North Bend. Thereafter they travelled in four, rolling parallel." Stocking, *The Road To Santa Fe,* 45.

35. "Kings of Georgia": These were young health-seekers from the state of Georgia mentioned in an article in the *St. Louis Missouri Republican,* October 16, 1856, as follows: "From the Plains: Among the arrivals yesterday were the Messrs. King, of Georgia, who have been spending the summer in hunting, &c, on the plains and mountains of the Far West. They bring no news. On the 2nd Inst. they met Maj. Simonson and officers with their detachment of rifles, at the Big Bend of the Arkansas, all well" (page 2). Interestingly, in July 1852 William Bent had artfully defied an ill-tempered party of Kiowas and Comanches determined to rob a trader named King whose nine-wagon train was a short distance behind Bent's caravan. Lavender, *Bent's Fort,* 323. Larkin mentions that these Kings went out to the plains with Bent in search of health and stayed at the New Fort, suggesting that they may have been related to Mr. King above.

36. Soda Spring: This refers to the hot and mineral springs at the entrance to Ute Pass, near present Manitou and Colorado Springs, Colorado. See Jones, *Health-Seekers In The Southwest,* 160; and Baur, "The Health Seeker in the Westward Movement, 1830–1900," 104.

37. Little Arkansas River: The Little Arkansas River enters the Arkansas at present Wichita, Kansas, and the trail crossed the small stream in present Rice County. Gregg, *Commerce of the Prairies,* 39, n. 5.

38. Chaves's murder: Here Larkin refers to the famous story of

trader Don Antonio José Chaves. Texan filibusters commanded by John McDaniel killed Chaves and robbed him of a quantity of gold in February 1843. The incident outraged the U.S. government and the Santa Fe traders and became part of the legendry of the trail. Gregg, *Commerce of the Prairies,* 337–38. The most recent treatment of this incident is Marc Simmons, *Murder on the Santa Fe Trail: An International Incident,* 1843.

39. Cow Creek: Cow Creek enters the Arkansas River at Hutchinson, Kansas, but the crossing was near present Lyons.

40. Arkansas River: The principal river in the region. From this point on to Bent's Fort, Larkin will follow the course of the Arkansas.

41. Walnut Creek: Walnut Creek enters the Arkansas about four miles east of present Great Bend, in Barton County, Kansas.

42. Booth & Allison: Francis Booth and William Allison, formerly stage conductors for Waldo, Hall and Company, opened Allison and Booth's Walnut Creek Station, or "Allison's Ranche," probably in 1856. Taylor, *First Mail West,* 42. The *Santa Fe Weekly Gazette,* October 31, 1857, page 3, carried a brief story indicating that an unidentified "Mexican" who was subsequently arrested had murdered a "Mr. Booth" of Walnut Creek with an axe. A man named only "Booth" appears in David Meriwether's account of his tenure as governor of New Mexico Territory from 1853 to 1857. In 1855 Meriwether evidently convinced Dr. Michael Steck, recently appointed as Indian Agent for the Territory, to cancel his reservation on the Independence-Santa Fe stage and go instead with the governor on horseback. Jacob Hall, the proprietor, was not offended but his conductor, "Booth," was enraged at Meriwether for depriving him of a passenger and "wanted to break down [Meriwether's] team and hoped the Indians would scalp [Meriwether]." Meriwether, *My Life in the Mountains and on the Plains,* 190 ff. Morris Taylor recounts the same story and identifies Booth. Taylor, *First Mail West,* 37–38.

43. Cheyenne Indians: Here Larkin first meets the tribe with which William Bent was associated for almost forty years. The diary passage on pp. 28–29 demonstrates that Yellow Woman

took care to watch out for Larkin and that she wielded influence over the young Cheyenne men in the party that visited Bent's train.

44. Incident at Fort Laramie: Here Larkin refers to events that occurred about one year after the 1855 "Mormon Cow" incident and the Grattan massacre, both of which involved the Sioux. In April 1856 the Northern Cheyennes became embroiled with the army at Fort Laramie over horses alleged to have been stolen from a white man. In a brief affray three Cheyennes were killed or captured, and one escaped to tell his people of the incident. As a result the Northern Cheyennes moved down to the Platte and Arkansas rivers to join their southern brethren. In August cavalry units from Fort Kearny attacked a Cheyenne camp on Grand Island, killing several and capturing horses and equipment, because a few warriors had molested the monthly mail train. The Cheyennes, having experienced "two unprovoked attacks," wreaked havoc on the Platte Road until September, when the disturbances ceased. The following spring, 1857, Colonel E. V. Sumner, First Cavalry, undertook the first United States punitive expedition against the Cheyennes and by September 1857 had confiscated the Cheyenne's annuity goods and given them to the Arapahos. This explanation follows George Bent's account of the events. Hyde, *Life of George Bent*, 98–105. See note 50, below.

45. Fort Atkinson: Located on the bank of the Arkansas River about two miles west of present Dodge City, Kansas, and 165 miles west of Council Grove, Fort Atkinson was only intermittently occupied between 1851 and 1854. Robert W. Frazer, ed., *Mansfield on the Condition of the Western Forts*, 13.

46. Crossing of the Arkansas: This is the "Upper Crossing" of the Arkansas River, near Chouteau's Island. Gregg, *Commerce of the Prairies*, 49.

47. Hilles: Larkin's brother, Eli Hilles Larkin is here referred to. See note 9 on Eli Hilles Larkin in "In Search of Better Health," above.

48. Chouteau's Island: Located on the upper ford of the Arkan-

sas River, in Kearney County near present Hartland, this island took its name from an incident that occurred in 1816 when fur trader Auguste P. Chouteau and his party were obliged to take cover on the island to ward off an attack by Pawnees. Gregg, *Commerce of the Prairies*, 19, n. 22.

49. Bent's Fort: Bent's New Fort, built in 1853, and occupied until 1860, when William Bent leased the fort to the Army. Mumey, *Bent's Old Fort and Bent's New Fort on the Arkansas River* has the most detailed treatment of the site and an illustration of Bent's New Fort. Larkin's description of the fort is one of the best on record, and he stayed at the fort longer than any journalist known to me.

50. Cheyenne troubles at Fort Kearny: On September 22, 1856, the *St. Louis Daily Missouri Democrat* printed a report extracted from the *Council Bluffs Bugle*, September 9, 1856, entitled "Startling News from the Plains." The article recounted a story of a Cheyenne attack on a government wagon train under contract to a Colonel A. W. Babbitt, led by a Mr. Nichols, during which several men were killed. Similarly, the *St. Louis Missouri Republican* on September 19, 1856, printed an item dated the 9th from Fort Leavenworth concerning a Cheyenne raid on the Oregon mail about twelve miles from Fort Kearney, and on the same day, a four-wagon train of a Mr. "Babbitt of Utah." See note 44, above.

51. Vogle from Westport: Unidentified, except perhaps for passing references to a John W. Vogel [sic] in Mumey, *Bent's Old Fort and Bent's New Fort on the Arkansas River*, 143, and to a Westport man named Vogel in Parkman's *The Oregon Trail*, Francis Parkman, *The Oregon Trail* (Garden City, N.Y.: Doubleday & Company, 1946), p. 7. The "Frenchman" remains unidentified.

52. Harper's Magazine: Larkin had with him a copy of the September *Harper's New Monthly Magazine*, 13:76 (Sept 1856), 455–72, containing an extensive review of James P. Beckwourth's *Life and Adventures of Jas. P. Beckwourth, Mountaineer, Scout and Pioneer; and Chief of the Crow Nation of Indians* (New York: Harper

and Brothers, 1856). The book was reviewed in the *St. Louis Daily Missouri Democrat* on September 13, 1856, just a few days before Larkin returned to St. Louis from his eastern health trip.

53. arrival of Bent's train at the fort: This event occurred on October 22, though the rapid advance party of Bent, Larkin, and a few others had arrived on October 13.

54. Humming tops and jumping jacks: Here is a reference to some unusual Indian trade items that demonstrates William Bent's inventiveness in selecting goods, or his sharp sense of how best to realize a profit.

55. shooting party: Larkin had done a bit of practicing on October 18, which may have prepared him for the competition here indicated. Not only was Larkin a good marksman, but he also appreciated fine rifles. He had paid $29.00 for one of Samuel Hawken's famed plains rifles (Larkin's trail inventory is included as Appendix 1). Hawken ran continual advertisements in two dailies in St. Louis, and his shop was located near Larkin's house.

56. Bent's livestock brand: Here is the only recorded description of William Bent's brand known to me.

57. Greenhorn Mts: Also called the Wet Mountains. Greenhorn Peak in Colorado is 12,347 feet high, and lies about sixty miles northwest of the Bent's Fort Branch of the Santa Fe Trail. The peak was named after Cuerno Verde, a Comanche chief killed in the vicinity during a battle with Spaniards under governor of New Mexico Juan Bautista de Anza in 1779. Janet Lecompte, *Pueblo, Hardscrabble, Greenhorn: The Upper Arkansas, 1832–1856* (Norman: University of Oklahoma Press, 1977), 31.

58. Purgatory River: El Rio de Las Animas Perdidas en Purgatorio (The River of Lost Souls in Purgatory), or "Picketwire" of the Mountain Men, which the Bent's Fort branch of the Santa Fe Trail crossed at present Trinidad, Colorado. Lavender, *Bent's Fort*, 13.

59. John Smith: This is John Simpson Smith (1810–1871), called "Blackfoot John" by his trapper comrades. Smith was an excellent linguist and found work as an interpreter after he quit trapping in the early 1830s. Ann W. Hafen could not fix Smith's

whereabouts between 1854 and 1857, and his appearance in Larkin's diary helps place Smith in New Mexico during 1856–57. Ann W. Hafen, "John Simpson Smith," in Hafen, ed., *Mountain Men and the Fur Trade*, 5: 325–45.

60. Bent's Old Fort: Bent's Old Fort, built in 1833, was the most famous landmark on the southern plains until after the Mexican War. Abandoned in 1849, in favor of Bent's New Fort about thirty-five miles down the Arkansas River, near present Lamar, Colorado, Bent's Old Fort played a significant role in the American occupation of New Mexico in 1846 and has received much more attention than its successor. Interestingly, Larkin indicates that a few persons still used the decaying fort, countering authorities who have stated that William Bent (or Indians) ruined the fort in 1849. Seven years later part of the fort was still in usable condition. See also an illustration attributed to Seth Eastman in 1869 that shows Bent's Old Fort with occupied quarters, functional chimneys, and chickens and swine outside the walls. Patricia Trent and Peter H. Hassrick, *The Rocky Mountains: A Vision For Artists in the Nineteenth Century* (Norman: University of Oklahoma Press, 1983), plate 7, p. 19.

61. Wahtahyah: Here Larkin refers to the Wah-To-Yah, or Spanish Peaks, made famous by Lewis H. Garrard's *Wah-to-yah, and the Taos Trail*, first published in 1850. The highest of the two peaks is 13,626 feet above sea level, and they lie about seventy miles from the point where Larkin observes them. Lewis Hector Garrard, *Wah-to-yah, and the Taos Trail; or Prairie Travel and Scalp Dances, With a Look at Los Rancheros from Muleback, and the Rocky Mountains Campfire* (Cincinnati: H. W. Derby, 1850).

62. Rio Timpas: The Timpas, a small stream entering the Arkansas near La Junta, Colorado.

63. 3 Buttes: The Three Buttes are prominent landmarks still visible today on U.S. highway 350, a few miles southwest of Timpas, Colorado, to the east of the present road bed. Marc Simmons notes that "the stage route of the SFT passed through a gap between them and the adjoining hills on the west side." The desolate stretch of highway between La Junta and Trinidad retains

some of its character from trail days. Simmons, *Following the Santa Fe Trail,* 132.

64. crossing of the Timpas: Evidence indicates this crossing to have been about eight miles downstream from Hole-in-the-Rock. See note 65 below.

65. Hole in the Rock: Located about one mile from present Thatcher, Colorado (and about fifty-five miles southwest of Bent's Old Fort), the Hole-in-the-Rock was a fissure that constituted the headwaters of the Timpas Creek and offered valuable water even during times of drought on the trail. Simmons, *Following the Santa Fe Trail,* 133.

66. Hole in the Prairie: Hole-in-the-Prairie was about fifteen miles southwest of the Hole-in-the-Rock and was known to have good water and grass. Taylor, *First Mail West,* 117, 213, n. 11.

67. Pike's Peak: Visible on clear days from where Larkin noticed it, the peak overlooking present Colorado Springs is 14,110 feet in elevation and lies about 100 miles to the north.

68. Turkey hunt: Perhaps this was the only opportunity Larkin had to use the shotgun he carried in his wagon. See inventory in Appendix 1 for shotgun and accessories.

69. Road over Raton Pass: In 1866 "Uncle Dick" Wootton at his own expense built and opened a toll road over the pass lying at an elevation of 7834 feet. Larkin's estimate of the cost was probably not far off, but no records remain. Richens Lacy Wootton (1816–1893) began his career in the Santa Fe trade with Bent, St. Vrain & Co., in 1836. Still active in 1856, he took a thirty-six-wagon caravan from Fort Union to Kansas City. Perhaps Larkin saw his train during his travels, but since Wootton and Bent were friends it is unlikely that a meeting would have escaped Larkin's notice. Duffus, *The Santa Fe Trail,* 234, and Harvey L. Carter, "Dick Wootton," in Hafen, *Mountain Men and The Fur Trade,* 3: 397–411.

70. Canadian River: Larkin would have crossed the Canadian river near the future site of the Clifton House, built between 1866 and 1870. Simmons, *Following the Santa Fe Trail,* 138.

71. Rio Vermejo: A branch of the Canadian River.

72. Cimarron: Cimarron would be the site for Lucien B. Maxwell's mansion, built about 1864; but when Larkin saw the site, only a few of Maxwell's employees, and possibly Kit Carson, lived there. Judging from Larkin's diary, Cimarron was apparently a camp for hunters.

Mr. Maxwell: Lucien Bonaparte Maxwell (1818–1875), legendary trapper, Indian trader, and New Mexico land baron. At the time Larkin met him, Maxwell had passed the nadir of his life and was beginning to amass a great fortune. In about 1848, Kit Carson loaned Maxwell one thousand dollars to inaugurate their joint ranching venture at Rayado, on the Beaubien-Miranda Grant. By 1865, Maxwell would complete the purchase of the grant from his father-in-law, Beaubien, and become the nation's largest individual land holder. Construction on his home at Cimarron probably began in 1862. During Larkin's stopover, Maxwell seems to have been living at Rayado. Harvey L. Carter, "Lucien Maxwell," in Hafen, *Mountain Men and The Fur Trade*, 6: 299–306.

73. Kit Carson: Two years later, Carson's first laudatory biography would appear. Peters, *The Life and Adventures of Kit Carson.*

74. Rial: Called Rial in Larkin's diary, Rayado was established by Lucien B. Maxwell in 1847 or 1848. In 1850 a small military garrison occupied Rayado to serve as protection for traders' caravans on the trail between Raton and Las Vegas. Simmons, *Following the Santa Fe Trail*, 145–46. According to Larkin's diary, he passed through Cimarron first, and then went to Rayado, where he stayed at Maxwell's house for one night. Note that Robert W. Frazer says "When Fort Union was established in 1851, Maxwell moved to Cimarron, where he erected a new house similar to his house on the Rayado," but Larkin's diary indicates that Maxwell still lived at Rayado in 1856. Frazer, *New Mexico in 1850*, 138, n. 35. D. L. Magruder was stationed at Rayado in 1850, his first army post. Frazer, *New Mexico in 1850*, 145.

75. Moro: Mora, New Mexico, was officially founded in 1835, although the site had been intermittently occupied since about 1820. George P. Hammond, *The Adventures of Alexander Barclay, Mountain Man*, 59, 65n.

76. Col. St. Vrain: Ceran St. Vrain (1802–1870) had been one of the organizing partners of Bent, St. Vrain & Company in about 1832. By 1850 St. Vrain was no longer in business with William Bent, the sole survivor of the original four Bent brothers. St. Vrain moved from Taos to Mora in 1855, and during Larkin's visit to New Mexico, he was engaged in politics, land speculation, and flour milling. Harold H. Dunham, "Ceran St. Vrain," in Hafen, *Mountain Men and The Fur Trade*, 5: 297–316.

77. José Play: Joseph or José Pley was the son-in-law of Stephen Louis Lee, the sheriff of Taos who was killed along with Governor Charles Bent and others during the Taos revolt of 1847. José Pley inherited Lee's share of the Sangre de Cristo Grant which, unbelievably, he sold to Carlos Beaubien "for one hundred dollars, in order to pay Lee's debts." David J. Weber, "Stephen Louis Lee," in Hafen, *Mountain Men and The Fur Trade*, 3:187. In 1848, Pley bought a still from Alexander Barclay and was in 1852 accused with Barclay and Joseph Doyle of selling whiskey to troops at Fort Union. At the time Pley had a contract to deliver corn to the fort. José Pley was the principal figure in Mora, active as merchant, flour miller and distiller. He eventually sold the mill and distillery to Ceran St. Vrain. Hammond, *The Adventures of Alexander Barclay*, 100, 105, n. 38; 206, n. 119.

78. W. A. Bransford: William Bransford was a merchant living at Mora. He seems also to have made money freighting for others. "On the 18th, Mr. Bransford, with a train of eleven wagons freighted with merchandize for the Messrs. Speigelberg arrived." *Santa Fe Weekly Gazette*, June 20, 1857.

79. fandango: Waltz & baluner[?]: Larkin attended his first of many fandangos at Mora. He was clearly not a tobacco smoker, as evidenced by his negative reaction to the smoke-filled room in which the event took place. The meaning of the word that appears to be "baluner" is unclear.

80. Mr. Fisher: Unidentified. Perhaps the reference to Fisher selling "so many saints" indicates that he vended either small religious medals or the lithographic prints that were common among Catholics.

81. troops sent to Bent's Fort: William Bransford has just informed Larkin that trouble had erupted at Bent's Fort and that Fort Union had received Bent's request for aid between November 8 and 11. Larkin had arrived at Bent's New Fort on October 13 and left on October 26. In this regard, the *St. Louis Missouri Republican* printed a notice on December 28, 1856, entitled "From Santa Fe and the Plains" that noted: "Bent has recently had some difficulty with the Kiowas, and was compelled to shoot two of them, for which act the bands threatened to take revenge, and it was only by the aid of the Cheyennes that he escaped molestation." A few weeks later, the *Santa Fe Weekly Gazette* published the following information excerpted from an article that appears in full in Appendix 2:

The command under Lt. McRae, Rifles, returned to Fort Union from Bent's Fort, on the 8th inst[ant] . . . On the 9th of September last, "Sitting Bear," a Kiowa chief, with fifty, or sixty men . . . went to the Fort and forced the man in charge to give him two barrels of sugar, and seven, or eight barrels of hard bread, of the subsistence stores there deposited. . . . On the 26th October [the day Larkin departed the fort for Santa Fe] ten or twelve of the principal men (Kiowas) went to the Fort to have a "talk" with Mr. Bent—he told them to leave—"Eagle Tail," one of their chiefs, following him menacingly from room to room, Mr. Bent fired at him. . . . On the first November forty or fifty Kiowas came up, and commenced firing towards the Fort. The Cheyennes drove them off, wounding two.—On the 19th December "Sitting Bear," with a small party went to the Cheyenne village, near the Fort and tried to prevail upon the Cheyennes not to be at peace with the whites.

Larkin probably missed the worst of the hostilities at Bent's New Fort. Significantly, the newspapers make no mention of Bent's employee having illegally given whiskey to the Kiowas, and the story has taken rather a different texture. Larkin's diary indicates that the overt antagonisms commenced on October 13 and 14. If the trouble began in early September, it would have been while William Bent was en route to Westport. What for Larkin was an event that threatened personal harm had become inflated in the press to the level of a broader crisis.

82. convent in Santa Fe: Reverend Jean Baptiste Lamy, who arrived to assume the bishopric at Santa Fe in 1851, inaugurated the convent of the Sisters of Loretto. In 1852 he made a trip to St. Louis, and returned with four sisters who began the convent and academy of Our Lady of Light at Santa Fe. Twitchell, *The Leading Facts of New Mexican History*, 2: 328–35.

83. Las Vegas: Founded about 1835, Las Vegas was an important trail community of well over one hundred houses by 1856.

84. Padre of Las Vegas: The priest is identified as Francisco Pinal in an article from the *Santa Fe Weekly Gazette*, October 25, 1856, which notes: "We have been furnished with a few of the items of property taken by the Kiowas, near Las Vegas, on their late visit to our settlements. . . . On the 10th of September these Indians passed near Las Vegas and took seven head of sheep and goats, and destroyed a field of corn belonging to the priest Francisco Pinal of Las Vegas." The priest's name was Jean François Pinard. This man is not mentioned in Twitchell's *Leading Facts of New Mexican History* or in the comprehensive Fray Angelico Chavez, *Archives of the Arch-Diocese of Santa Fe, 1678–1900* (Washington, D.C.: Academy of American Franciscan History, 1957). For his identification, see n. 18, in "The Trail to Santa Fe," above.

85. paregoric: Here Larkin identifies the bottle of "pain killer" he listed in his inventory. See Appendix 1.

86. Tecaloté: When Frederick Wislizenus saw it in 1846, Tecoloté was comprised of about thirty houses. Frederick A. Wislizenus, *Memoir of a Tour to Northern Mexico*, 17.

87. Moore & Rees: A note in the *Santa Fe Weekly Gazette*, June 20, 1857, indicates that "the train of Messrs. Moor Rees and Co, of Tecaloté, reached that place on the 7th inst[ant]." No additional information on these men is extant.

88. San Miguel and its Hotel: San Miguel del Bado (San Miguel of the Ford), at the Santa Fe Trail crossing of the Pecos River, about forty miles southeast of Santa Fe. Twitchell says that San Miguel had about one thousand residents in 1850. Twitchell,

The Leading Facts of New Mexican History, 2: 130, n. 90. It is possible that the "hotel" Larkin speaks of may be the house of Thomas Rowland, brother of famed mountain man John Rowland, who had lived at San Miguel since about 1835 and certainly since 1839. Field, *Matt Field*, 251, 254–55; David J. Weber, "John Rowland," in Hafen, *Mountain Men and The Fur Trade*, 4: 275–81. Wislizenus found San Miguel to be "somewhat larger and wealthier than Las Vegas." Wislizenus, *Memoir of a Tour to Northern Mexico*, 18.

89. Ruins at and legend about Pecos: For a review of several variants of this legend consult Kessell, *Kiva, Cross and Crown*, 459–63.

90. Jim Grey's ranch, "Roseville": James or Santiago Gray was involved in a court proceeding at Taos in 1855 (District Court Records, Taos County, Criminal Cases, 1855, in State Archives Records Center). A Grey's Ranch existed on the Purgatory in southern Colorado, but this reference is to a different site, near Pecos, New Mexico. This writer has not seen it on a map, nor is it mentioned in Thomas M. Pearce, *New Mexico Place Names*.

91. cañon with hills on each side: Apache Canyon, site of the "battle that was never fought" when the Americans captured Santa Fe in 1846 and near the site where the battle of Glorieta Pass would occur in 1862.

92. Santa Fe: For an excellent contemporary description, see Russell, *Land of Enchantment*, especially pp. 31–57. Marian Russell left Santa Fe for Fort Leavenworth in August 1856, a few months before Larkin arrived.

93. the Fonda: A landmark of Santa Fe, the Exchange Hotel, or La Fonda, was under American ownership from 1846 onward. About 1850, Thomas Bowler and Frank Green bought the hostelry and operated it until 1865, when it sold to Thomas McDonald and John D. Baker. Peter Herzog, *La Fonda: The Inn of Santa Fe*. Unfortunately, Larkin failed to transcribe the slogans he noticed painted on the walls of the barroom, and they have appeared nowhere else.

94. Dr. Connelly's store: Doctor Henry Connelly ran a retail store on the plaza at Santa Fe. In 1842, Connelly had formed a partnership with Edward James Glasgow to conduct trade between Independence, Missouri, and Chihuahua, Mexico. Horn, *New Mexico's Troubled Years,* 94; also note 32, above.

95. Amberg and Brittingham: Jacob Amberg was in partnership with Henry Connelly, and Henry F. Brittingham was a clerk in the concern.

96. Mr. Miller: See note 109, below, in which David J. Miller is mentioned as a member of the Literary Club.

97. Mr. Beck; Beck, Johnson & Co.; Webb & Kingsbury: Preston Beck, Jr., was a leading merchant in Santa Fe who was mortally wounded in a knife fight with a John Gorman, an employee at Richard Owens's store in Santa Fe, on March 26, 1858. Gorman died immediately, but Beck lingered for some days before he expired. So well respected was he that a meeting of his friends was held at the court house on April 8 to prepare a series of resolutions concerning his untimely death. *Santa Fe Weekly Gazette,* March 27, April 10, 1858. Webb & Kingsbury were the preeminent traders in the city, and Larkin had letters to the firm from his cousins, Glasgow & Brother, of St. Louis.

98. Major Albert Smith and J. R. Triplett: Larkin here employs a letter for Smith from Triplett as a means for an introduction to Smith. Triplett is probably one of the principals of Triplett & Sells, St. Louis merchants who, like Thomas H. Larkin & Company, engaged in the hemp trade in that city. Triplett & Sells had an office at Lexington, Missouri. *St. Louis Missouri Republican,* September 13, 1856.

99. Mr. Green: This man is Frank Green, who with Thomas F. Bowler, purchased the Fonda hotel at Santa Fe. Note that Larkin seems to have arranged with Green for a cheaper rate at the hotel. Larkin ms. diary, 1856–57, 72.

100. Mr. Macrae: This appears to be Lieutenant Nathaniel C. Macrae, but the text is not clear, and this could be Mr. Mercer. See note 104, below.

101. Joab Houghton: Houghton (1811–1877) was born in New York, and went to New Mexico as a trader in 1844. He was appointed chief justice of New Mexico by Lt. Colonel Kearny in 1846, and served in that capacity for many years, despite his lack of legal expertise. He had been educated as a civil engineer, and eventually received a contract to design the uncompleted state house Larkin saw in Santa Fe. Twitchell, *The Leading Facts of New Mexican History*, 2: 272, n. 197.

102. Fort Marcy: Built in 1846, officially abandoned in 1894, its practical usefulness ended in 1851 with the establishment of Fort Union.

103. Indicated here are the following:
John D. Wilkins
Colonel Benjamin Louis Eulalie Bonneville
Major Thornton
Captain Langdon C. Easton
Lieutenant Henry B. Clitz
Lieutenant Howland
Lieutenant Lawrence W. O'Bannon
Major William A. Nichols
Governor David Meriwether
"Squire" James L. Collins

For those men named, except Meriwether and Collins, see Frazer, *New Mexico in 1850: A Military View*; Frazer, *Mansfield on the Condition of the Western Forts*. For David Meriwether, see Meriwether, *My Life in the Mountains and on the Plains*. James L. Collins (1800–1869) was from Kentucky, but went to New Mexico in 1826. From 1828 to 1846 he lived and traded in Chihuahua, returning to Santa Fe in 1846. In 1852 he inaugurated the *Santa Fe Weekly Gazette*, which he ran until 1858. In 1858 President James Buchanan appointed Collins Superintendent of Indian Affairs of New Mexico. Collins died under mysterious circumstances in 1869. Meriwether, *My Life in the Mountains and on the Plains*, 169n.

104. Mr. Mercer: As identified in Larkin's diary, this man was

Major Albert Smith's clerk. His full name was George D. Mercer, member of the Literary Club of Santa Fe. Larkin appears to have replaced Mercer as clerk.

105. Bishop's Church: This is the church east of the plaza in Santa Fe, formerly known as *La Parroquia,* later demolished to make way for Lamy's "Midi-romanesque" cathedral. Now called the Cathedral of San Francisco, or the cathedral of St. Francis de Assizi, the present edifice was built around the old walls of its Spanish Colonial predecessor. Building commenced in 1869 and continued for many years. Larkin saw the church as artist Richard H. Kern depicted it in 1849. Weber, *Richard H. Kern,* 136–39, and plate 8; Bruce T. Ellis, *Bishop Lamy's Santa Fe Cathedral,* plates 1 and 2.

106. Mrs. Wilkins and Mrs. Macrea: Military wives, Mrs. Lieutenant Nathaniel C. Macrae, and Mrs. Lieutenant John D. Wilkins.

107. the mail arrived today: This is the monthly Independence-to-Santa Fe mail.

108. grand agricultural fair, St. Louis: Chapter above comparing St. Louis and Santa Fe notes this event that occurred during October 1857 at St. Louis. See also *St. Louis Daily Missouri Democrat,* September 17, 1856.

109. Literati Club; Empire Club: Officers and Merchants formed a Literary Club early in 1856 to hold debates and morally edifying discussions. Examples of debate topics included: "As Aaron Burr was arraigned and tried for the crime of treason, should not Messrs. Hale, Sumner and Giddings be arraigned and tried for treason also?" and "Does the Territory of New Mexico offer sufficient inducements to immigration?" However, when the club petitioned W. W. H. Davis, secretary of the Territory, for the "contemplated incorporation by the Legislature of said club," Davis ridiculed the idea. The infuriated members quickly responded with a letter printed in the *Weekly Gazette* excoriating Davis for his "insulting, dirty, and intensely vulgar language" and refused to have any dealings with him. *Santa Fe Weekly Gazette,* November 11, December 13, 25, 1856. Members of the Club

included William Drew, president; Leonidas Smith, secretary; David J. Miller, treasurer; Col. John B. Grayson, guardian of essays; Henry F. Brittingham, Jesús Sena y Baca, N. M. Macrae, C. P. Clever, George D. Mercer, A. P. Wilbar, and Charles E. Whilden. No reference to the Empire Club has surfaced.

110. Chatto & Juana Armijo: Larkin met Don Salvador Armijo of Albuquerque, known also to Franz Huning as Chatto, a variant of Chato, or "flat-nose." Huning, *Trader On the Santa Fe Trail*, 58.

111. Concert by 3rd Infy Band: The Third Infantry Band apparently arrived in Santa Fe early in October 1856. The *Santa Fe Weekly Gazette*, October 11, 1856, noted "We understand that the band of the 3rd infantry is to remain in this city during the winter, this will be a pleasure quite unexpected by our citizens, and for which they are indebted to Colonel Bonneville, who is the Colonel of that regiment. The band is said to be an excellent one." Larkin attended several performances of the band while in Santa Fe.

112. Dr. Cavanaugh: Finis E. Cavanaugh, of Santa Fe.

113. Story about recruits and their muskets: Lieutenant Charles E. Whilden, whom Larkin met in Santa Fe, was an observer of this event and wrote a letter describing it to his family. About mid-July 1855, the Third Infantry was en route to New Mexico, and Whilden, a native of Charleston, South Carolina, was on hand to witness a prairie fire that caused many rifles to discharge, wounding several and killing one. Charles E. Whilden, "Letters From A Santa Fe Army Clerk, 1855–1856", 143.

114. Court Martial of Capt. McLean: A notice in the *Santa Fe Weekly Gazette*, December 8, 1856, reported: "A general court martial will convene in this city, on the 10th instant, for the trial of Brevet Captain McLane of the mounted Rifles, on charges preferred against him by Lt. Ransome of the same regiment. The following named officers will compose the court. Col. Loring, Col. Miles, Col. Grayson, Col. Porter, Maj. Holmes, Maj. Van Horn, Maj. Crittenden, Maj. Kendrick, Maj. Thornton, Capt. Easton, Capt. Sykes, Captain Rhet, Capt. Jones, and Doctor Sloan,

Judge Advocate. Lt. Ransome arrived in town on the 20th ultimo." No information has appeared defining the charges brought against McLean, but the court sat until at least December 13.

115. Mr. Boyce, of Las Vegas: The *Santa Fe Weekly Gazette,* January 17, 1857, noted that there had "Died at Las Vegas, New Mexico, on the 11th inst. Henry Stephen Boyce, infant son of Dr. Stephen and Helen Boyce, of that village."

116. Fort Union, New Mexico: Lieutenant Colonel Edwin Vose Sumner established Fort Union in July 1851 near Las Vegas, where the Mountain and Cimarron branches of the Santa Fe Trail converged. Undertaken in part to remove the troops from the vice-ridden capital, the post served as the center for Ninth Military Department operations against the Indians, and also saw service during the Civil War before it was decommissioned in 1891. The principal work on the site, now a National Monument, is Emmett, *Fort Union and the Winning of the West.*

117. Blanc Mange: A sweet pudding made of cornstarch, or flour, and cream.

118. Mr. Beck a passenger to the States: The mail coach, with a few passengers aboard, left Santa Fe on January 4, 1857, but met severe weather and the carriers were forced to abandon their wagon near Walnut Creek. The *Santa Fe Weekly Gazette* reported that "Mr. Beck of this city was a passenger with the mail bound for the states, and although he had suffered greatly, we are happy to learn that he was so far recovered, as to be able to continue his journey east." *Santa Fe Weekly Gazette,* March 6, 1857.

119. Mexican Funeral: In 1849 Franz Huning described such an affair: "There was a custom among the people then, that when a child died, the parents hired a fiddler, who sat down by the side of the little body and played all day long every waltz and other dances that he had ever played at the fandangos, also church music, all mixed up. They said that the child was an angel now, and that angels loved music." Huning, *Trader On The Santa Fe Trail,* 25.

120. J. W. Dunn & Spanish Classes: J. W. Dunn began to advertise his services as a teacher of English and Spanish, for

males or females, in the November 15, 1856 issue of the *Santa Fe Weekly Gazette.* The notice read: "We publish today, on the Spanish side of our paper, the card of Mr. J. W. Dunn, announcing the commencement of his school. Mr. Dunn proposes to teach both the English and the Spanish scholars, for which we have reason to believe him well qualified. . . . Mr. Dunn has comfortable rooms in the house now owned by the Rev. Mr. Shaw, and we have no doubt, he will be mindful of the comfort of the children intrusted to his care."

121. Eastern and Southern Mails: Larkin refers here to the monthly Independence-Santa Fe and the San Antonio (Texas)–Santa Fe mail coaches, which also carried a few passengers. Due to bad weather and Indian threats, the mails were often behind schedules, as the diary and newspaper articles indicate. See note 119, above.

122. Mr. Idler of Placer Mining Co.: A "Mr. Idler" arrived at Santa Fe with the Independence mail on October 23, 1856, as the "agent and general director of the mining company organized some time since in Washington City, to work the Placer gold mines near this place." *Santa Fe Weekly Gazette,* October 25, 1856. Eugene Leitsendorfer and other Jewish merchants were involved with the concern. "A Visit to the Placer Mines," *Santa Fe Weekly Gazette,* October 18, 1856.

Bibliography

Archives

City of St. Louis Census Records
City of St. Louis Probate Court Records
Joint Collection: University of Missouri, Western Historical
    Manuscript Collection/Columbia State Historical Society of
    Missouri Manuscripts
Missouri Historical Society, St. Louis
    William Carr Lane Collection
    Joseph Mullanphy Papers
    Sublette Papers
    Charles van Ravenswaay File
    James Josiah Webb Collection

Newspapers

St. Louis Daily Missouri Democrat 1856–57
St. Louis Globe-Democrat 1918, 1937
St. Louis Missouri Republican 1856–57
Santa Fe Weekly Gazette 1856–57

Bibliography

Articles

Baur, John E. "The Health Seeker in the Westward Movement, 1830–1900," *Mississippi Valley Historical Review* 46 (June 1959), 91–110.

Becknell, William. "The Journals Of Capt. *Thomas* [sic] Becknell From Boone's Lick To Santa Fe, And From Santa Cruz To Green River," *Missouri Historical Review* 4: 2 (January 1910), 65–84.

Bernard, William R. "Westport and the Santa Fe Trade," *Transactions of the Kansas State Historical Society,* 1905–1906, 9: 552–65 (Topeka: State Printing Office, 1906).

Carson, William G. B. "Secesh," Missouri Historical Society *Bulletin* 23: 2 (January 1967), 119–45.

Chappell, Phil. E. "A History of the Missouri River," *Transactions of the Kansas State Historical Society,* 1905–1906, 9: 237–294 (Topeka: State Printing Office, 1906).

——— "Missouri River Steamboats," *Transactions of the Kansas State Historical Society,* 1905–1906, 9: 295–316 (Topeka: State Printing Office, 1906).

Cruise, John D. "Early Days on the Union Pacific," *Transactions of the Kansas State Historical Society,* 1905–1906, 9: 529–49 (Topeka: State Printing Office, 1906).

Field, Ruth K. "Some Misconceptions About Lucas Place," Missouri Historical Society *Bulletin* 20: 2 (January 1964), 119–23.

Greene, Albert R. "The Kansas River—Its Navigation," *Transactions of the Kansas State Historical Society,* 1905–1906, 9: 317–58 (Topeka: State Printing Office, 1906).

Griffith, B. W. E. "The Battle of Black Jack," *Collections of the Kansas State Historical Society,* 1923–1925, 16: 524–28 (Topeka: Kansas State Printing Plant, 1925).

Lamar, Howard R. "Rites of Passage: Young Men and Their Families in the Overland Trails Experience, 1843–69," in *"Soul Butter and Hog Wash," and Other Essays on the American*

Bibliography

West, Thomas G. Alexander, ed., (Provo: Brigham Young University Press, 1978), 33–67.

Möllhausen, H[einrich] B[alduin]. "Over the Santa Fe Trail Through Kansas in 1858," *Kansas Historical Quarterly* 16: 4 (November 1948), 337–80.

n.a. "Explanation of Map," *Transactions of the Kansas State Historical Society*, 1905–1906, 9: 565–78 (Topeka: State Printing Office, 1906).

Olch, Peter D. "Treading the Elephant's Tail: Medical Problems on the Overland Trails," *Bulletin of the History of Medicine*, 59 (1985), 196–212.

Stadler, Francis Hurd, "Letters From Minoma," Missouri Historical Society *Bulletin*, 16: 3 (April 1960), 237–59.

Utley, Robert M. "Fort Union and the Santa Fe Trail," *New Mexico Historical Review* 36: 1 (January 1961), 36–48.

van Ravenswaay, Charles. "Years of Turmoil, Years of Growth: St. Louis in the 1850s," Missouri Historical Society *Bulletin* 23: 4 (July 1967), 303–24.

Whilden, Charles E. "Letters From A Santa Fe Army Clerk, 1855–1856", ed. by John Hammond Moore, *New Mexico Historical Review* 40: 2 (April 1965), 141–64.

Wyman, Walker D. "Freighting: A Big Business on the Santa Fe Trail," *Kansas Historical Quarterly* 1: 1 (November 1931), 17–27.

——— "Kansas City, Mo., a Famous Freighter Capital," *Kansas Historical Quarterly* 6: 1 (February 1937): 3–13.

Books

Abert, Lieutenant James W. *Report of an Expedition led by Lieutenant Abert on the Upper Arkansas and Through the Country of the Comanche Indians, in the Fall of the Year 1845 . . . Journal of Lieutenant J. W. Abert, from Bent's Fort, on the Arkansas River, Saturday, August 9, 1845.* U.S. Congressional Documents, Vol. 477, 29th Cong., 1st Sess., Senate Exec. Doc. 438, Washington, D.C., 1846. Reprinted as John Galvin, ed., *Through the Country of the Comanche Indians In The Fall Of The Year 1845* (San Francisco: John Howell Books, 1970).

Bancroft, Hubert Howe. *The Works of Hubert Howe Bancroft*, vol. 18, *History of Arizona and New Mexico, 1530–1888* (San Francisco: The History Company, 1889).

Barry, Louise, ed. *The Beginning of the West: Annals of the Kansas Gateway to the American West, 1540–1854* (Topeka: Kansas State Historical Society, 1972).

Berkebile, Don H. *Carriage Terminology: An Historical Dictionary* (Washington, D.C.: Smithsonian Institution Press, 1978).

Brown, William E. [*The Santa Fe Trail.*] *The National Survey of Historic Sites and Buildings Series, Theme XV: Westward Expansion and Extension of the National Boundaries, 1830–1898; The Santa Fe Trail* (Subtheme). (Washington: United States Department of the Interior, National Park Service, 1963). Reprinted: Patrice Press, 1989.

Catlin, George. *Letters and Notes on the Manners, Customs, and Condition of the North American Indians* (New York: Wiley and Putnam, 1841).

Chaput, Donald. *François X. Aubrey: Trader, Trailmaker and Voyageur in the Southwest* (Glendale: Arthur H. Clark Company, 1975).

Chavez, Fray Angelico. *Archives of the Arch-Diocese of Santa Fe, 1678–1900* (Washington, D.C.: Academy of American Franciscan History, 1957).

Compton, R. J., ed. *Pictorial St. Louis; A Topographical Survey Drawn in Perspective, 1875* (St. Louis: n.p., c. 1876).

Connor, Seymour V. and Skaggs, Jimmy M. *Broadcloth and Britches: The Santa Fe Trade* (London and College Station: Texas A & M University Press, 1977).

Cullum, George W. *Biographical Register of the Officers and Graduates of the U.S. Military Academy at West Point, New York* (New York: Van Nostrand, 1868).

Davis, William Watts Hart. *El Gringo: or, New Mexico and Her People* (New York: Harper & Brothers, 1857).

Bibliography

Drumm, Stella M., ed. *Down the Santa Fe Trail and into Mexico, the Diary of Susan Shelby Magoffin; 1846–1847* (New Haven: Yale University Press, 1927).

Duffus, Robert L. *The Santa Fe Trail* (New York: Longmans, Green and Company, 1930).

Ellis, Bruce T. *Bishop Lamy's Santa Fe Cathedral: The Records of the Old Spanish Church (Parroquia) and Convent Formerly on the Site* (Albuquerque: University of New Mexico Press, 1985).

Emmett, Chris. *Fort Union and the Winning of the Southwest* (Norman: University of Oklahoma Press, 1965).

Encyclopaedia Britannica, 9th ed. (New York: Charles Scribner's Sons, 1882).

Fender, Stephen. *Plotting the Golden West: American Literature and the Rhetoric of the California Trail* (Cambridge: Cambridge University Press, 1981).

Field, Matthew W. *Matt Field on the Santa Fe Trail*. Collected by Clyde and Mae Reed Porter, edited by John E. Sunder (Norman: University of Oklahoma Press, 1960).

Frazer, Robert W. *Forts of the West* (Norman: University of Oklahoma Press, 1965).

——, ed. *Mansfield on the Condition of the Western Forts* (Norman: University of Oklahoma Press, 1963).

——, ed. *New Mexico in 1850: A Military View* (Norman: University of Oklahoma Press, 1968).

Garrard, Lewis Hector. *Wah-to-yah, and the Taos Trail: or Prairie Travel and Scalp Dances, with a Look at Los Rancheros from Muleback, and the Rocky Mountains Campfire* (Cincinnati: H. W. Derby & Co., 1850).

Goetzmann, William H. *Exploration and Empire: The Explorer and the Scientist in the Winning of the American West* (New York: Alfred A. Knopf, 1966).

Gould, E. W. *Fifty Years on the Mississippi: Or, Gould's History of River Navigation* (St. Louis: Nixon-Jones Printing Company, 1889).

Gregg, Josiah. *Commerce of the Prairies: or the Journal of a Santa Fe Trader, during Eight Expeditions across the Great Western Prai-*

ries, *and a Residence of nearly Nine Years in Northern Mexico,* 2 vols. (New York: Henry G. Langley, 1844; reprint edited by Max Moorhead, Norman: University of Oklahoma Press, 1954).

Gregg, Kate L., ed. *The Road to Santa Fe: The Journals and Diaries of George Champlin Sibley* (Albuquerque: University of New Mexico Press, 1952).

Hafen, LeRoy R. and Hafen, Ann W., eds. *Relations with the Indians of the Plains, 1857–1861. The Far West and the Rockies Historical Series,* 15 vols. (Glendale: Arthur H. Clark Company, 1959).

Hafen, LeRoy R., ed. *Mountain Men and the Fur Trade,* 10 vols. (Glendale: Arthur H. Clark Company, 1965–72).

Hammond, George P. *The Adventures of Alexander Barclay, Mountain Man* (Denver: Old West Publishing Company, 1976).

Herzog, Peter. *La Fonda: The Inn of Santa Fe* (Santa Fe: Press of the Territorian, 1964).

Hodge, Frederick Webb, ed. *The Handbook of American Indians North of Mexico.* Bureau of American Ethnology, Bulletin 30 (Washington, D.C.: Government Printing Office, 1906).

Hoig, Stan. *The Sand Creek Massacre* (Norman: University of Oklahoma Press, 1961).

Horn, Calvin. *New Mexico's Troubled Years: The Story of the Early Territorial Governors* (Albuquerque: Horn & Wallace, 1964).

Huning, Franz. *Trader On The Santa Fe Trail: The Memoirs of Franz Huning.* Notes by Linda Fergusson Browne (Albuquerque: Calvin Horn Publisher, Inc., 1973).

Hyde, George E. *Life of George Bent, Written From His Letters.* Edited by Savoie Lottinville (Norman: University of Oklahoma Press, 1968).

Ingraham, Prentiss, ed. *Seventy Years On The Frontier: Alexander Majors' Memoirs of a Lifetime on the Border* (Chicago and New York: Rand, McNally & Company, 1893, reprint ed. Minneapolis: Ross & Haines, 1965).

Inman, Henry. *The Old Santa Fe Trail: The Story of a Great Highway* (New York: The Macmillan Company, 1897).

Jones, Billy M. *Health-Seekers In The Southwest, 1817–1900* (Norman: University of Oklahoma Press, 1967).

Kennerly, William Clark (as told to Elizabeth Russell). *Persimmon Hill: A Narrative of Old St. Louis and the Far West* (Norman: University of Oklahoma Press, 1948).

Kessell, John L. *Kiva, Cross and Crown: The Pecos Indians and New Mexico 1540–1840* (Washington: National Park Service, Government Printing Office, 1979, reprint edition Albuquerque: University of New Mexico Press, 1987).

Lamar, Howard R. *The Far Southwest: 1846–1912: A Territorial History* (New Haven: Yale University Press, 1966).

————, ed. *The Reader's Encyclopedia of the American West* (New York: Thomas Y. Crowell Company, 1977).

Lavender, David. *Bent's Fort* (Garden City, N.Y.: Doubleday, 1954).

Lecompte, Janet. *Pueblo, Hardscrabble, Greenhorn: The Upper Arkansas, 1832–1856* (Norman: University of Oklahoma Press, 1977).

Meriwether, David. *My Life in the Mountains and on the Plains*. Edited and with an introduction by Robert A. Griffen (Norman: University of Oklahoma Press, 1965).

Meyer, Duane. *The Heritage of Missouri: A History* (St. Louis: State Publishing Company, 1963).

Moorhead, Max L. *New Mexico's Royal Road: Trade and Travel on the Chihuahua Trail* (Norman: University of Oklahoma Press, 1958).

Mumey, Nolie. *Old Forts And Trading Posts of the West: Bent's Old Fort and Bent's New Fort on the Arkansas River* (Denver: Artcraft Press, 1956).

n.a. *The St. Louis Directory For The Years 1854–5* (St. Louis: Chambers & Knapp, 1854).

Oliva, Leo E. *Soldiers on the Santa Fe Trail* (Norman: University of Oklahoma Press, 1967).

Bibliography

Pearce, Thomas M. *New Mexico Place Names: A Geographical Dictionary* (Albuquerque: University of New Mexico Press, 1965, reprinted 1975).

Peters, DeWitt C., M.D. *The Life and Adventures of Kit Carson, The Nestor of The Rocky Mountains* (New York: Clark & Meeker, 1859).

Pike, Albert. *Prose Sketches and Poems Written in the Western Country* (Boston: Light and Horton, 1834, reprint ed. by David J. Weber, Albuquerque: Calvin Horn Publishers, 1967).

Rittenhouse, Jack D. *The Santa Fe Trail: A Historical Bibliography* (Albuquerque: University of New Mexico Press, 1971).

Russell, Marian. *Land of Enchantment: Memoirs of Marian Russell Along the Santa Fe Trail*, as dictated to Mrs. Hal Russell. Edited by Garnet M. Brayer, Afterword by Marc Simmons (Albuquerque: University of New Mexico Press, 1981).

Sadie, Stanley, ed. *The New Grove Dictionary of Music and Musicians*. 20 vols. (London: MacMillan Publishing, 1980).

Salpointe, J. B. *Soldiers of the Cross, Notes on the Ecclesiastical History of New Mexico, Arizona, and Colorado* (Banning, Ca.: St. Boniface's Industrial School, 1898).

Simmons, Marc. *Following the Santa Fe Trail: A Guide For Modern Travellers* (Santa Fe: Ancient City Press, 1984).

———. *Murder on the Santa Fe Trail: An International Incident, 1843* (El Paso: Texas Western Press, University of Texas at El Paso, 1987).

———, and Joan Myers. *Along the Santa Fe Trail* (Albuquerque: University of New Mexico Press, 1986).

Spidle, Jake W., Jr. *Doctors of Medicine in New Mexico: A History of Health and Medical Practice, 1886–1986* (Albuquerque: University of New Mexico Press, 1986).

Stocking, Hobart E. *The Road To Santa Fe* (New York: Hastings House, 1971).

Taylor, Morris F. *First Mail West: Stagecoach Lines on the Santa Fe Trail* (Albuquerque: University of New Mexico Press, 1971).

Trenton, Patricia, and Hassrick, Peter H. *The Rocky Mountains: A*

Vision For Artists in the Nineteenth Century (Norman: University of Oklahoma Press, 1983).

Twitchell, Ralph Emerson. *The Leading Facts of New Mexican History.* 2 vols. (Cedar Rapids: Torch Press, 1912).

Unruh, John D., Jr. *The Plains Across: The Overland Emigrants and the Trans-Mississippi West, 1840–60* (Urbana: University of Illinois Press, 1978).

Utley, Robert M. *Fort Union National Monument, New Mexico* (Washington: Government Printing Office, 1962).

Vexler, Robert I., compiler and editor. *St. Louis: A Chronological & Documentary History, 1762–1970.* American Cities Chronology Series, Series editor Howard B. Furer (Dobbs Ferry, N.Y.: Oceana Publications, Inc., 1974).

Wade, Richard C. *The Urban Frontier: The Rise of Western Cities, 1790–1836* (Cambridge: Harvard University Press, 1959).

Walker, Henry Pickering. *The Wagonmasters: High Plains Freighting from the Earliest Days of the Santa Fe Trail to 1880* (Norman: University of Oklahoma Press, 1966).

Webb, James Josiah. *Adventures in the Santa Fe Trade, 1844–1847,* ed. by Ralph P. Bieber, Southwest Historical Series, vol. I (Glendale: Arthur H. Clark Company, 1931).

Weber, David J. *Richard H. Kern: Expeditionary Artist in the Far Southwest, 1848–1853* (Albuquerque: University of New Mexico Press, 1985).

Wislizenus, Frederick A. *Memoir of a Tour to Northern Mexico, Connected With Col. Doniphan's Expedition, in 1846 and 1847.* Senate Miscellaneous Documents, No. 26, 30th Congress, 1st Session. (Washington: Tippin & Streeper, 1848, reprinted as Frederick A. Wislizenus, *A Tour to Northern Mexico 1846–1847,* Glorieta: Rio Grande Press, 1969).

Index

Beck, Preston, Jr., 103, 107,
 114, 127, 128(n.1),
 174(n.97), 178(n.111)
Beck, Johnson & Co., 103,
 118, 119, 132, 174(n.97)
Becknell, William, 7,
 138(n.6)
Bellefontaine Cemetery, 21,
 28
Bent, Charles (brother of
 William), 153–54(n.2),
 170(n.77)
Bent, Charles (son of
 William), 158(n.15)
Bent, George (brother of
 William), 153–54(n.2)
Bent, George (son of
 William), 150–51(n.11),
 164(n.44)
Bent, Robert (brother of
 William), 153–54(n.2)
Bent, William, 158(n.15);
 trader, 1, 6, 57, 59, 68,
 73, 81, 88, 89, 90, 119,
 126, 138(n.4), 153–
 54(n.2), 166(n.54),
 167(n.60); guide, 4, 27,
 70; character, 55, 56, 82,
 120; Indian disturbances,
 58–59, 83–85, 129–32,
 171(n.81); brand, 60, 89,
 166(n.56); hunter, 74, 75,
 78; Indian relationship, 77,
 162(n.35), 163(n.43);
 family, 6, 55, 58, 73, 78,
 150(n.11), 153–54(n.2),

160(n.26), 170(n.76)
Bent's Fort, 6, 10, 60, 68,
 80, 91, 138(n.4),
 150(n.11); description, 81–
 90, 165(n.49); Kiowa
 disturbance, 27, 43, 56,
 58, 59, 61, 74, 83–85, 99,
 129–32, 171(n.81);
 distance, 154(n.4),
 167(n.60)
Bent's New Fort. *See* Bent's
 Fort
Bent's Old Fort, 59, 60, 91,
 154(n.4), 167(n.60),
 168(n.65)
Bent's Old Fort National
 Historic Site, 8–9,
 138(n.3), 146(n.27)
Bent, St. Vrain & Co.,
 168(n.69), 170(n.76)
Bernalillo, 107
Bernard, James, 157–58(n.15)
Bernard, William R.,
 150(n.11), 154(n.2), 157–
 58(n.15)
bilious fevers. *See* dysentery
Bluff Creek, Kansas, 73
Bonneville, Benjamin Louis
 Eulalie, 104, 110, 118,
 175(n.103), 177(n.111)
Boomer, G. B., 105, 106
Boomer & Hynes, 105
Boone, A. G., 150(n.11),
 154(n.2), 158(n.15)
Boone & Bernard, 158(n.15)
Booth, Francis, 76, 163(n.42)